DIGGING FOR INSIGHTS

Using Archaeology to Study the Bible

John F. Brug

Northwestern Publishing House
Milwaukee, Wisconsin

Cover Illustrations: Lars Justinen
Interior Illustrators: John Brug, Glenn Myers
Art Director: Karen Knutson
Designer: Pamela Dunn

Northwestern Publishing House
1250 N. 113th St., Milwaukee, WI 53226-3284
www.nph.net
© 2010 by Northwestern Publishing House
Published 2010
Printed in the United States of America
ISBN 978-0-8100-2233-1

TABLE OF CONTENTS

PREFACE

How does archaeology help us understand the Bible? What are its strengths and its limitations? How can we learn to evaluate the claims that archaeologists make about the Bible? How can we evaluate archaeology critically, that is, distinguish data from interpretation and speculation? These are some of the questions we will attempt to address in this volume.

After speaking about the methods and contributions of archaeology in general, we will consider what archaeology can teach us about various aspects of life in biblical times. We will then conclude with some warnings against bias and misuse of archaeology, both by supporters and critics of the Bible.

All of the chapters are summaries, designed for the non-professional, with very limited footnotes and documentation. For the most part, these summaries are based on popular reports rather than technical studies. Some of the more technical material has been placed in the appendices. Additional reading is suggested at the ends of chapters and in the final bibliography. Measurements are usually rounded off from meters to feet and from grams to pounds.

What is archaeology? What do archaeologists do? Most people have little idea. If they have a notion, it is likely to be far removed from reality. If the average person on the street were asked to name a famous archaeologist, he or she might name a movie "archaeologist" like Indiana Jones, or Rick O'Connell and Evie Carnahan-O'Connell, or maybe Lara Croft, tomb raider. They often imagine whip-cracking heroes rescuing beautiful women or being rescued by them. Or they recall archaeologists battling ancient curses from the mummies they have disturbed, fighting evil Nazis bent on controlling the world, and finding mounds of jewels and gold. Maybe they even find treasures with magic powers like the ark of the covenant or the holy grail. What a life!

The reality, of course, is quite different. Real archaeologists seldom find treasures of silver and gold. (A fabulous treasure hoard has never been found in Israel, and even in Egypt there has been only one, the tomb of King Tut.) Archaeologists rarely, if ever, have to engage in running gun battles with evil rivals. Their major hardships are enduring hot, dirty conditions while digging and spending long hours at a desk studying and publishing their finds. For the most part, their finds are rows and piles of stones, various colors of dirt, and tons of broken pottery. Ancient people seldom left good things behind, and when they did, it was almost never on purpose. What archaeologists find are mostly the ruins: the rejects and the wreckages of life. In short, archaeology is sorting through people's garbage in a systematic, scientific way.

The Study of Ancient Things

The word *archaeology* means the study of ancient things. In the narrow sense, archaeology is the discovery and analysis of the material remains of ancient cultures. The term is sometimes used in a wider sense, which includes the study of written records from the past. In this sense it overlaps with ancient history. Since some of the written records of ancient times were recovered by archaeological excavations, we will touch on such documents briefly, but in this book we will be concerned primarily with the physical remains from ancient cultures, such as buildings, tombs and graves, sewers and toilets, pottery, tools and weapons, coins, and idols.

As we are using the term here, *archaeology* first of all refers to a method for recovering the past. Second, it refers to the data and interpretations produced by that method.

Some archaeological treasures are discovered accidentally by construction workers digging ditches or intentionally by thieves and looters rummaging through archaeological sites, but we would not call bulldozing sites or robbing tombs archaeology. *Archaeology* is a carefully planned recovery of ancient remains. We may define it as the recovery of the past by systematically discovering, recording, preserving, analyzing, and publishing remains that have survived from past civilizations. Biblical archaeology is applying the results that are obtained by such methods to the study of the Bible.

To carry out a successful archaeological project, an archaeologist (or more likely a team of archaeologists) needs a site to excavate; a set of goals for the excavation; a plan for the excavation; permission to excavate the site; a support staff of supervisors, workers, and researchers; and enough money to fund the project. A more detailed summary of this process is provided in appendix I. It is important to read this to be aware of the limitations of archaeological methods.

Before we consider specific contributions of archaeology to the study of the Bible, we must consider in a more general way the strengths and weaknesses of archaeology as a tool for Bible study.

The Limitations of Archaeology

Though it can provide some verification of historical persons and events, archaeology does not prove or disprove the Bible. By and large, it cannot provide the type of information to do that. It can show that a city was destroyed at Jericho, but it normally does not provide information about who did it or whether it happened in a natural earthquake or a divinely timed one. Many people and events in the Bible are not of the type that would make much of an impression in the archaeological record. The patriarchs, for example, who are extremely important persons in biblical history, were not great kings who left vast palaces. Also, Jesus' ministry would not have produced a lot of archaeological evidence.

One of the greatest weaknesses of archaeology in reconstructing history is that it works with very limited evidence. Books often cite "the 2 percent rule." Archaeologists excavate 2 percent of the area of 2 percent of the sites and find 2 percent of what was once there. In destructions of sites, often all that remains are ruins, broken pottery, and anything that was not worth carting away. The evidence thus is relatively skimpy, and what remains is often jumbled. The site may have been damaged by erosion, quarrying, the mining of the site for building materials that could be reused, and the leveling of previous strata to prepare for new construction. In trying to reconstruct the history of the site, the archaeologist has only a tiny fraction of the evidence.

A second weakness is that the published results of the excavation contain a great deal of subjective interpretation. Some of this is inevitable because of the relatively sparse evidence. One of the most important things for readers of this book to learn is how to distinguish the evidence from the interpretation of the evidence. The evidence, for example, might be some burned buildings and broken pottery. Assigning a date to the building and suggesting how the building was destroyed is interpretation, often strongly influenced by written records or the excavator's biases. Two experts looking at the same data may produce very different interpretations. The interpretations may be influenced by the archaeologists' presuppositions and pet theories (theological or archaeological). An archaeologist who approaches the data looking for evidence to support a preconceived notion is likely to find it. (See chapter 11 for further discussion of the role of bias in archaeology.)

Sometimes other factors compound the uncertainty of interpretation. Even the identity of the site may be uncertain (for example, the locations of Bethel and Ai are disputed). All dating methods have their limitations. The archaeologist may be approaching the data with faulty assumptions or may be misled by faulty data or bad interpretations from previous excavations. We will try to provide specific examples in the chapters that follow.

The biases of archaeologists mean that even the very phrase *biblical archaeology* is now the subject of debate. Many archaeologists are embarrassed to have the name of their discipline associated with the Bible—too religious and unsophisticated for them. Others, of course, have a great interest in the Bible and may even have a specific aim of corroborating at least the basic historicity of the Bible. This latter view, of course, is much out of favor with the archaeological establishment today. Excavations undertaken with openly stated biblical aims are rare today. If archaeologists have specific biblically oriented goals, in most cases these would not be publicly acknowledged. This is a great change from the early 20th century when excavations with a specific biblical agenda were undertaken by Christian archaeologists such as William Albright and his school. Israeli archaeologists, even the secular, were very interested in biblical history as part of the heritage of their people. Very few of these men and women had a high view of the inerrancy of Scripture, but they believed the Bible had a basic historical core.

The ascent of negative critical views of Scripture has had a great impact on archaeology. Most archaeologists today accept moderate to extremely critical views of the Bible. The school known as minimalists, which believes that virtually nothing in the Old Testament is historical, influences a much larger segment of archaeology today than it did in the past. It is clear that some are trying to distance themselves from the embarrassment of a fundamentalist or orthodox past. Those who work in the academic world seek respectability and may bend to professional peer pressure. Sometimes the motivation is not anti-religious but simply a turn away from a primarily historical interest to more scientific and anthropological interests. Much support for archaeology in Israel still comes from people and institutions with a biblical interest. But the recent change of name of the periodical *Biblical Archaeologist* to *Near Eastern Archaeology* is a fitting indication of the shift from the overtly biblical archaeology of the early 20th century toward the historical minimalism in archaeology of the 21st century. Today new archaeological applications to the Bible will come more often from "arm-chair applications" of data obtained by secularly motivated excavations rather than from those undertaken with a specific biblical interest.

Archaeology can deal only with physical remains. It cannot evaluate spiritual things. For example, it can provide evidence that Jerusalem was destroyed around 586 B.C. and again around A.D. 70, but it cannot provide any evidence for the spiritual meaning of these events as judgments of God. Even in explaining the earthly causes of these events, we are almost entirely dependent on written records from the time.

Consider the archaeological evidence for two men, Herod the Great and Jesus of Nazareth. We have abundant evidence of the greatness of Herod in his palaces at Masada and his burial site at the Herodium. Traces remain of his great works at Caesarea and Samaria. Even though the temple he built was destroyed, the temple platform that remains is dramatic proof of his greatness as a builder. What would be the evidence for the great works of Jesus? The upper room that Jesus borrowed for the Last Supper has vanished. The evidence of his resurrection would be an empty tomb, of which there are many in Jerusalem. Nothing that remains today would show why the tomb was empty. The evidence of his crucifixion would be three barely traceable postholes in the ground. And yet Herod is gone and by and large forgotten, known by most for nothing except killing the babies of Bethlehem. The result of Christ's work endures, not because of physical remains that it has left but because of the work of the Spirit through the Word that remains.

Tutankhamen, a.k.a. King Tut, a short-lived pharaoh who was mediocre at best, left what is perhaps the most fabulous treasure trove ever found. The baby of Bethlehem left only an empty manger in a deserted stable. Yet the effect that this baby has on the world is immeasurably greater than that of King Tut.

We should not expect too much from archaeology since it cannot deal with the most important issues in the Bible. Nevertheless, it is not without value. In Israel few treasures are found, mostly foundations and pottery. But they contribute to the understanding of history and daily life. Archaeological findings provide much corroboration and amplification to the Bible, but many disputed cases remain, for example, at Jericho and Ai. At Jericho the dating of the ruins is disputed. The site of Ai is uncertain. We will continue our exploration of this problem in the following sections and chapters.

The Contributions of Written Records

The contributions of archaeology to the understanding of the Bible lie in two areas: the recovery of written records from the past and the recovery and analysis of artifacts from the material culture of ancient civilizations. The rest of this chapter will focus on the contributions of written records.

INSIGHTS INTO HISTORICAL EVENTS AND PERSONS

Until the 1800s our knowledge of ancient history in the Middle East was almost entirely dependent on the Bible and on the surviving writings of Greek and Roman authors. Knowledge of the languages of the ancient Near East, such as Egyptian and Akkadian (the language family to which Assyrian and Babylonian belong), had been lost. During the 1800s, as European nations began to become more involved in the Near East, there was new interest in the surviving monuments and documents of those areas. This led to the decipherment of Egyptian hieroglyphics and of the cuneiform writing of the Babylonians and the Assyrians. Now these languages could be read again, and a new window was opened into the history of the ancient Near East.

Many of the thousands of surviving documents recovered by archaeologists have no direct relevance for understanding the Bible. Many of them are simply bills and receipts or other economic records. Many have to do only with local events in Egypt or Mesopotamia.

Some of these documents do, however, help with the understanding of the Bible. They do this in three ways:

1. Some confirm the existence of people and events mentioned in the Bible and provide more information about them.
2. Some help us in our understanding of biblical Hebrew.

3. Some help us understand the culture and customs of biblical times.

Recovering such documents is the contribution of the archaeologist. Translating and interpreting these documents is the work of linguists and historians. We will not deal with the work of linguists and historians here, except for listing a few examples of the results of their work.

One of the most dramatic of these discoveries is the account of Sennacherib, king of Assyria, that tells of his campaign against the cities of Judah and Jerusalem. The biblical report of these events is recorded in 2 Kings chapters 18 and 19. The biblical account tells how, as a result of Hezekiah's rebellion, Sennacherib came up and attacked and captured the cities of Judah. After Hezekiah unsuccessfully tried to buy his way out of the mess he had gotten himself in, Sennacherib came up to besiege Jerusalem. As the Lord had promised, an angel of the Lord destroyed the Assyrian army in one night.

Now we can compare the biblical account with Sennacherib's own account as found on a prism (memorial pillar) uncovered in Assyria.

> As for Hezekiah, the Judean, who had not submitted to my yoke, I besieged 46 of his fortified walled cities and surrounding small towns, which were without number. Using packed-down ramps and by applying battering rams, infantry attacks by mines, breeches and siege machines, I conquered them. I took out 200,150 people, young and old, male and female, horses, mules, donkeys, camels, cattle and sheep, without number, and counted them as spoil. [Hezekiah], I locked him up within Jerusalem, his royal city, like a bird in a cage. I surrounded him with earthworks, and made it unthinkable for him to exit by the city gate. His cities which I had despoiled, I cut off from his land and gave them to Mitinti, king of Ashdod, Padi, king of Ekron and Silli-bel, king of Gaza, and thus diminished his land. I imposed upon him in addition to the former tribute, yearly payment of dues and gifts for my lordship. (Annals of Sennacherib, III, 18-37)

Sennacherib's account and the biblical account agree in all respects, including that neither of them reports the fall of Jerusalem. The only difference is that Sennacherib's account gives no reason for the omission of the fall of Jerusalem, which would have been the highlight of his campaign had it occurred. It is quite natural that in a monument erected to glorify himself, he would report his successes, not the disaster brought on by his arrogance against the Lord.

As an added bonus, excavation of Sennacherib's palace uncovered large wall carvings that picture the capture of Lachish, one of the cities of Judah. We see the assault on the city and the Judean captives being tortured, killed, or deported to Assyria. The siege ramp pictured in the carvings still exists at the site of Lachish.

There are similar parallel accounts for the war between Israel and Mesha, king of Moab. The biblical account in 2 Kings chapter 3 tells how, after the death of Ahab, Mesha rebelled against Israel. The kings of Israel and Judah led a campaign against Moab, which defeated the Moabite army and was at the point of capturing the king's city when Mesha sacrificed his firstborn son on the wall of the city and the Israelites withdrew.

In 1868 a stele (memorial stone) was discovered in Jordan by missionary F. A. Klein that gives Mesha's account of the war in the Moabite language. This black stone monument, which was about 4 feet high and 2 feet wide, was broken into pieces by the Arabs who had it in their possession. Some of the pieces were lost, but a copy of the text had been made before the stone was broken. A re-creation of the stone, which incorporates the original pieces that have survived and reproductions of the lost pieces, is on exhibit at the Louvre in Paris. This is an abbreviated version of Mesha's account:

> I am Mesha, son of Kemoshyat, the king of Moab, the Dibonite. My father was king over Moab for thirty years, and I became king after my father. . . . Omri, king of Israel— he oppressed Moab many days, because Chemosh was angry with his land. And his son succeeded him, and he also said, "I will oppress Moab." In my day he spoke according to this word, but I saw my desire upon him and upon his house, and Israel utterly perished forever. Now Omri had possessed all the land of Medeba and dwelt in it his days and half the

days of his son, forty years, but Chemosh restored it in my day. The men of Gad dwelt in the land of Ataroth from of old, and the king of Israel built there the city of Ataroth; but I made war against the city and took it. And I slew all the people of the city, for the pleasure of Chemosh and of Moab. And Chemosh said to me: "Go take Nebo against Israel"; and I went by night and fought against it from break of dawn till noon, and I took it and slew all, seven thousand men, boys, and women, and girls, for I had devoted it to Ashtar-Chemosh. And I took from there the altar-hearth of Yahweh, and I dragged it before Chemosh. And the king of Israel built Jabaz and dwelt in it while he fought with me, and Chemosh drove him out from before me.

As is typical of royal battle reports, Mesha reports the ultimate outcome of the war, which was Moabite independence, without mentioning the disastrous defeat along the way. The Israelite King Omri, whom Mesha mentions, was the father of Ahab. The "son" of Omri against whom Mesha revolts was actually the grandson of Omri. This stele thus confirms the historicity of Mesha, who plays a very minor role in the Bible, and provides Mesha's perspective on the same war reported in the Bible. It also confirms the biblical report that the tribe of Gad had remained in the Transjordan when Israel conquered the land (Numbers 32:3).

Most of the other historical accounts that parallel the Bible are less detailed or less specific than these two. We will mention a few of them here in passing.

Cuneiform letters found at Amarna in Egypt include diplomatic correspondence between the pharaoh and the kings of various city-states in Canaan, including Jerusalem during the period of the judges. Their portrayal of this era as a time of disorder corresponds quite well with the picture in Judges. There is no direct reference to the Israelites unless they are included among the Habiru, who are enemies of the Canaanite kings.

Accounts of Pharaoh Ramses III tell of land and sea battles against invaders that include the *plst*, who appear to be the biblical Philistines. This corresponds well with the biblical picture of the increased power of the Philistines near the end of the period of the judges. The accounts on the temple at Medinet Habu in Egypt are accompanied by pictures of the Philistines, who are wearing kilts and what appear to be feathered headdresses. Pictures of the Philistines in recent Bible story books are based on these Egyptian pictures of the Philistine invasion.

A stele of Pharaoh Merneptah reports the existence of Israel in the land of Canaan at about this same time.

Several kings of Israel and Judah appear in the annals of the Assyrian kings. The names and order of the kings of Assyria and Israel in these annals agree with the names and order in the Bible. The Black Obelisk of Shalmanesar contains what is apparently a picture of Jehu, king of Israel, bowing facedown and paying tribute.

Many critics of the Bible claim that David is a fictional character like King Arthur, but fragments of an Aramaic stele found at Dan, near the northern border of Israel, mention the house of David. This account fits well with the account of the wars between Israel and Aram in the book of Kings, though the details are unclear due to the fact that many pieces of the stele have not been recovered. The Moabite Stone of Mesha may also contain references to David.

Seal impressions found in the destruction layer of Jerusalem contain the names of a number of officials mentioned in the book of Jeremiah. A seal impression "Belonging to Hanan, son of Hilqiyahu, the priest" may refer to Hilkiah, the high priest during the reign of Josiah, king of Judah in the last part of the seventh century B.C. Yerahme'el, the son of the king, and Elishama, servant of the king, were officials during the reign of King Jehoiakim, who was a bitter adversary of Jeremiah (see Jeremiah chapter 36). The most interesting seal impression is that of Berchiahu, son of Neriahu, the scribe, who appears to be the Baruch, son of Neriah, who was Jeremiah's scribe. Baruch is a short form of the name Berchiahu, like Nathan for Jonathan. One of the two instances of this seal impression preserves a thumbprint. Recall the time when Baruch read the scroll of Jeremiah in the chamber of Gemariah, the son of Shaphan (Jeremiah 36:10). Might the seal impression "Belonging to Gemaryahy, son of Shaphan" and the thumbprint belong to this same man? Other surviving seals and seal impressions preserve names of biblical personages, including Jezebel and Hoshea.

In many cases it cannot be determined with certainty whether these seals belong to the biblical person or to someone else with the same name, although a seal with three points of correspondence—such as Baruch, son of Neriah, the scribe—seems to be too precise a match to be a coincidence.

The problem is compounded, however, by the fact that many of these seals and impressions were not discovered in excavations but turned up on the antiquities market as a result of chance finds or looting. They therefore cannot be reliably dated, and some may even be forgeries.

Cuneiform records help clarify the tumultuous last days of Babylon. Belshazzer, the king of Babylon at the time of its fall as recorded in Daniel, was the son of Nabonidus, an absentee king. This may cast light on why Belshazzer offered Daniel only third place in the kingdom and not second place.

The New Testament era is well documented by Greek and Roman historians, but occasionally some additional, interesting confirmations of biblical figures turn up. Excavations at Caesarea, the great city built by Herod, turned up a dedicatory inscription of Pontius Pilate.

More problematic is a pavement inscription from Corinth that refers to "Erastus, the *aedile* of the city." The office of *aedile* was the second highest office of the city. The *aedile* could perhaps be called the city manager. In Romans 16:23 Paul refers to a city official from Corinth, Erastus, whom he designates as the *oikonomos* of the city. The term *oikonomos* often refers to a household manager, but here Erastus, the officeholder, is called the *oikonomos* of the city. In commentaries and translations of Romans, *oikonomos* is rendered as "city treasurer" or "manager of public works." Many commentaries and books suggest that the Erastus in the pavement inscription and the Erastus that Paul mentions in Romans are the same man. However, *oikonomos*, Paul's term, is not the usual Greek equivalent for *aedile*. In Greek the *aedile* was called *agoronomos,* while *oikonomos* probably refers to one of the lesser financial offices, either *dispensator* or *arcarius.* Some commentators defend the identification of the two men by claiming that the man whom Paul knew as an *oikonomos* later ascended to the office of *aedile*. Others counter by saying that these respective offices would be held by men of quite different social status, so it is unlikely that the two offices would be held by the same person. In this case we cannot with certainty identify the man in the pavement inscription as the one in Paul's letter to the Romans.

In Jerusalem an ossuary (a stone box for the deposit of human bones after decomposition of the body) has been found with the name "Joseph, son of Caiapha." Historical records make clear that the high priest who tried Jesus had the personal name Joseph, and Caiaphas was a family name. It seems very probable that this is the high priest of Jesus' time or a near relative.

Much more disputed is an ossuary with the inscription "James, brother of Jesus." James, the brother of Jesus, was the leader of the Jerusalem church in the book of Acts. This box has caused vehement controversy on various grounds. Some are convinced this box refers to the James who plays a prominent role in Acts. Others vehemently deny this, either on the grounds that the combination of names is coincidental (both are common names) or that the inscription is in whole or in part a modern forgery. The controversy continues to rage on. It seems unlikely that either side will convince the other, though an Israeli court may have to rule on the charges of forgery (see chapter 12).

Cultural Insights

Other recovered writings throw some light on the culture of biblical times.

If archaeological dating is correct (see chapter 12), systems of writing, notably in Egypt and Mesopotamia, existed for more than 1,500 years before the writing of the first books of the Bible. But these systems of writing were very complicated, using hundreds of signs, much like Chinese. Becoming literate in such systems is very difficult. In alphabetic systems, readers have to learn only 20-35 signs. The earliest surviving alphabetic writing demonstrates that the alphabet was invented at just the right time and place to be used in the writing of the first books of the Bible in the middle of the second millennium B.C. Some of the earliest surviving alphabetic writing was found in the Sinai wilderness, although there is no evidence linking it to Israel. However, it may well be that the earliest books of the Bible were the first important literary works written in the alphabet. Our alphabet is a descendent of this first alphabet via Greek and Latin.

Although officials often used scribes to write down their words, the alphabetic graffiti from various periods of Old Testament history provide evidence that literacy was not limited to a scribal class.

There was another alphabet in use at this time that looked like cuneiform. This alphabet was used in northern Syria at the city of Ugarit. Linguistically this language died out and became a dead end. But study of the Ugaritic language helps us understand some of the features of archaic Hebrew, especially Hebrew poetry. Also, among the many texts from Ugarit are epics about Baal and other gods and goddesses. Though the Bible mentions Baal often, it says very little about him or his worship. The texts from Ugarit fill in some of the blanks.

The Dead Sea Scrolls deserve comment. They were first discovered by accident by Bedouin nomads, but they are classified as an archaeological find because of their antiquity and because subsequent finds of scrolls were the result of controlled archaeological excavations of caves near Qumran on the shores of the Dead Sea. Many of these scrolls (or in most instances, scroll fragments) preserve portions of Old Testament books in unpointed Hebrew. (Ancient Hebrew contained only consonants. The vowels were added later in the form of points.) Most of these portions of Scripture date from around the time of Christ or a little earlier. These were a thousand years older than the oldest Hebrew manuscripts then known. The great value of these scrolls is that their text is essentially the same as the text we have in the Hebrew Bible, which was produced from manuscripts copied a thousand years after the writing of the Dead Sea Scrolls. This provides important evidence for the careful copying and transmission of the Bible.

Examples of useful cultural evidence from literary sources more removed from the Bible are provided by Mesopotamian law codes, such as the Code of Hammurabi. The civil laws of Israel contained many parallels to this law code and others. For example, they contained laws on how to assess damages caused by an ox that gores (Exodus 21:28) or the use of a slave girl to act as a surrogate mother to produce a child for the chief wife of the family who might be barren—note Sarah and Hagar, Leah and Zilpah, Rachel and Bilhah. These similarities are not necessarily due to any direct influence from one code to another but to the natural knowledge of the law, which everyone has, and to the similar needs of similar cultures. For example, cultures that have lots of oxen must have provisions for what happens if an ox gores—that's what oxen do.

Sumerian and Akkadian records have flood accounts that bear some striking similarities to the biblical account. Again, this does not necessitate any direct influence from one text to the other, but it is evidence for the preservation of two streams of a common heritage: one stream in a garbled form through tradition, the other stream in a pure form through inspiration.

The topic of how other ancient literature sheds light on the Bible is a subject in its own right, which we cannot pursue in detail here. Archaeology has contributed to this knowledge by recovering many of the textual resources for this study. This is, in effect, a fringe benefit of archaeology.

In the chapters of this volume, we will focus our attention not primarily on the finds of ancient literature but on the physical remains recovered and interpreted by archaeology.*

*For more information on ancient texts, see: John H. Walton, *Ancient Israelite Literature in Its Cultural Context: A Survey of Parallels Between Biblical and Ancient Near Eastern Texts;* D. Winton Thomas, *Documents From Old Testament Times; J. B. Pritchard, Ancient Near Eastern Texts* (ANET); and William W. Hallo, *The Context of Scripture, Vol. 1: Canonical Compositions From the Biblical World* and *Vol. 2: Monumental Inscriptions From the Biblical World.*

POTTERY: ITS USES AND LIMITATIONS

2

Pottery is the most important object to be found during archaeological excavations in Israel. It is plentiful because of several characteristics that it has: it is so easily broken, it is so indestructible, and it was worth so little to those who broke it. Because it is so easily broken, pottery produces a lot of debris. Because it does not rust or decay, the broken pieces will remain in the ground until the world ends. Because baked clay is not recyclable as metal is, the shards of pottery were left behind in the ruins of sites, often at the very spots where the pots were broken.

In the Bible, man is often compared to pottery. He is a jar shaped by God, the potter. But like a clay jar, he is easily broken and returns to the ground he came from. In the grave, like the lifeless broken pieces of clay, he is worth nothing. In the lifeless, broken pieces of clay that littered the ground all around him, the Israelite saw a picture of human weakness and mortality. In his prayer of agony, the Messiah in Psalm 22:15 says:

> My strength is dried up like a potsherd,
>> and my tongue sticks to the roof of my mouth.

Of the exiled King Jehoiachin, Jeremiah asks:

> Is this man Jehoiachin a despised, broken pot,
>> an object no one wants?
>> Why will he and his children be hurled out,
>> cast into a land they do not know? (Jeremiah 22:28)

But the useless, broken pots assume great value when recovered by the archaeologist. They become the most important objects in the reconstruction of the site's history. Among their many uses are dating the strata of the site, providing evidence for the use of rooms, giving some indication of the technology of the society, assisting in cultural analysis, and providing evidence of trade and migration.

The Chronology of Strata

By far the most important use of pottery is in dating the various levels of the site. Through careful study of the millions of pieces of pottery found in excavations, archaeologists have created a calendar of sorts that can be used to date strata (layers) in a site. In the same way that you could assign scattered pages of high school yearbooks to the right decade from the hairstyles, glasses, and clothing of the students pictured, archaeologists can date strata of an excavation by the styles of pottery found in it.

The process of pottery dating is complicated. As a starting point, archaeologists need some dateable loci (plates) with a good sampling of pottery. (See appendix I for a description of loci in archaeological excavation.) These loci can be assigned a date on the basis of other criteria, such as dateable coins, dateable inscriptions, and so on. Layers immediately above and below the dateable layer can then also be assigned approximate dates. Using this yardstick, loci and strata from other sites that contain the same style of pottery as the dateable loci are dated to the same time period. An elaborate system of chronological benchmarks is then developed and is being constantly refined. An archaeologist then compares the pottery from various levels of his site with this chronological yardstick and assigns calendar dates to the loci of his site. To go back to our earlier comparison: if I have established that a certain number of pages from a high school yearbook show the styles of the 1950s, I can with a fair degree of confidence assign other pages that I receive to the same time period on the basis of their similarity to the first pages that were reliably dated.

Nevertheless, there is a degree of vagueness and uncertainty in this process. Since pottery styles may be much more long-lived than modern clothing or hairstyles, pottery dating is much less precise than yearbook dating. Often archaeologists are only able to narrow down the time period to a century or a portion of a century. Also, the archaeologist has to be careful that his or her sample is adequate. If a building has been destroyed and a number of pots have been crushed in place on the floor by the collapse of the building, the dating is quite reliable. But a few stray sherds in a locus do not enable one to date the locus because they may be remnants of a much earlier time period. In such cases we can say that the locus is no older than the most recent sherd it contains but cannot say much more. In reality, many loci of a site are dated by their relationship to a few dateable loci that lie above or below them.

Pottery Typology

Pottery typology is the art of establishing a series of types of pottery that can be used as benchmarks of certain time periods. The shape of the vessels, the quality and treatment of the clay, and the decorations are among the features that are used in this effort to establish recognizable types. Whole vessels, whether found intact or restored from broken pieces, are of course most useful, but the type and date of vessels can often be identified from a few "diagnostic" pieces. Rims, bases, and handles of vessels are called diagnostic sherds since they are much more easily associated with a certain type and time than undecorated, plain body sherds.

Since pottery typology is more easily understood from pictures or drawings (or, even better, from handling the pottery), we will describe only a couple of pottery types.

First, oil lamps. Oil lamps began as bowls into which wicks were placed to give light. Early in the biblical period, at the time of the patriarchs, the lamps were bowls that had been folded in on four sides to produce a vessel with four spouts.

Through most of the Old Testament period, lamps were bowls that were pinched in one place to produce one spout into which a wick was placed. This style continued for centuries, but as time passed, the pinch of the spout became tighter, the rim of the bowl became more flared out, and the base became flatter and higher. So although the basic style remained the same, there was a dateable progression.

Near the end of the Old Testament time period, there was a distinct change in style. Lamps became closed vessels with small openings in the top for the wick and for pouring in the oil. This style continued through the New Testament time period. But here too there were distinct subtypes within the style. Types from different time periods are distinguished by the shape of the body and the spout, by the presence or absence of handles, and by finish and decorative elements.

Cooking pots from various eras are distinct. Cooking pots from the earliest biblical periods are flat-bottomed and circular. Later they have no base but are round bottomed with carinated (bent) sides and made of a more gritty red ware. The shaping of the rim is also diagnostic of different periods.

The same type of development and dating charts can be developed for other types of pottery, such as large storage jars or small juglets. Reference works to be used in dating pottery contain many drawings of whole vessels and diagnostic sherds to provide the archaeologist with some points of comparison for dating his materials. These, however, are no substitute for extensive experience in handling and studying the pottery types themselves.

Other Uses of Pottery

In addition to its use as a dating tool, pottery can make many other contributions to the understanding of a site.

THE USE OF ROOMS

Since rooms have often been destroyed almost to ground level and perishable items are long gone, pottery is often the only evidence for the use of rooms. The presence of a lot of large storage jars indicates a food storage area, and in larger numbers it may indicate a storage room or warehouse. A lot of cooking and serving vessels identify the food preparation area. Many misshapen pottery rejects, called wasters, identify a pottery manufacturing site. A large collection of vessels used in worship marks a shrine or, if found in large numbers and within an appropriate architectural form, a temple (see chapter 5).

THE TECHNOLOGY OF SOCIETY

The remains of pottery also provide evidence of technological proficiency. How well was it made? Was a pottery wheel used, or was it crudely manufactured by hand? Was the clay well refined? Was the pottery well fired? This, however, is not evidence of the overall technology of a culture. What we might consider a rather primitive culture may have invested a lot of care and effort to produce high quality pottery. A rather advanced culture may have been satisfied with utilitarian disposables. A rather low-grade pottery may be evidence of a prioritizing of resources (not wanting to use a lot of fuel for high quality firing) rather than a lack of technological ability. It is interesting that for the most part, Israel was content with rather plain, drab pottery that was not especially well manufactured.

CULTURAL ANALYSIS

Pottery forms may include idols and other religious items, toys, artwork, and equipment for the manufacture of other items (such as a special form of vessel used for spinning yarn). Strainer jars may indicate a preference for beer over wine. Pottery may preserve artwork of plants and animals, geometric designs, war scenes, myths and stories, or religious scenes. As noted previously, this pictorial element is rather rare in Israelite pottery. It is, however, quite important in the pottery of Israel's neighbors—those near at hand like the Canaanites and Philistines and those far away, the Greeks in particular.

TRADE AND MIGRATION

Pottery styles also vary from culture to culture. Greek pottery found in Israel provides evidence of trade. In large amounts containing many forms, it may provide evidence of foreign groups migrating to the area. This analysis, however, is not without its hazards. If pottery with a clear foreign influence arrived in Israel, did the potters move or merely the pots? The presence of a few luxury goods in a foreign style is probably no more than evidence of trade. The arrival of a whole repertoire of items, including everyday ware like cooking pots, may indicate the arrival of immigrants. Even when there is an increase of foreign luxury wares, one must distinguish actual imports from locally produced imitations. Imitations can sometimes be distinguished by analysis of the method of manufacture (just as modern "knockoffs" of designer fashions may be). Was the maker using the same techniques as the foreign manufacturer or simply creating a visual reproduction of an import using his or her own techniques? Tests of the trace elements can determine whether or not the clay from which the pottery was made was local.

In this respect, the Philistine Ware of the end of the second millennium B.C. often comes under discussion. This decorated pottery includes shapes and decorative motifs that are obviously derived from Mycenaean (Greek) styles. The pottery of the Philistine sites at this time also includes non-Canaanite forms of utilitarian ware, such as cooking pots. This pottery was clearly made locally in Philistia. Other foreign elements are also present in the Philistine culture. There are, however, some significant differences between the local Philistine Ware and the Mycenaean prototypes. For example, the painting and finish of Philistine monochrome (one color) and bichrome (two color, black and red on white) pottery is less lustrous than that of Mycenaean ware. Overall the evidence points to Philistine migration (a fact that is directly stated in the Bible)—very likely not directly from the Greek Aegean but probably by way of Cyprus. It also points to a culture that was amalgamating diverse elements on its way toward a high degree of assimilation into the local culture of Canaan. The whole topic is more complex than we can deal with here, but the point is that the first archaeological evidence suggesting a connection of the Philistines with the Greek world was their pottery.

TRACES AND IMPRESSIONS OF MATERIALS LEFT ON THE CLAY

Storage jars may contain trace elements of the products that were once contained in them—oil, wine, kinds of spices or fragrances. This may provide evidence of trade patterns.

Processing of Pottery

The main steps of pottery processing are finding, recording, washing, restoring, drawing and publication, and display.

The first step is, of course, finding the pottery. Pottery is not usually found whole but shattered into pieces called sherds or shards. The best chance of finding intact pottery is in undisturbed tombs. Such tomb finds can produce a nice assemblage of pottery from one period or from a number of closely related periods, but it is not necessarily representative of the main types in daily use.

In some ways even more valuable is an assemblage found smashed but unscattered in a destruction layer. This gives good data for dating and produces restorable vessels. The recording process begins immediately as the pottery is placed in buckets and later in bags labeled as to where the pottery was found.

The pottery is then washed, usually on the afternoon of the day it is found. This serves a number of important purposes. It naturally keeps the storage bags clean. Clean pottery is easier to study. Clean pottery is easier to restore. But there is also an important fringe benefit to this process. Fairly flat body sherds from large vessels were the scratch paper of that day. Sherds used for this purpose are called ostraca. They were used to record financial transactions, to write letters or at least the drafts of letters, and for ballots. In the washing process, faded ink writing may be detected. The two most important finds of letters from ancient Israel, the letters from Lachish and Arad, were written on ostraca. These two sets of letters describe events during the last days of Judah, before the nation fell to Babylon. They are, therefore, contemporaneous with the account of these troubled times recorded in the book of Jeremiah. The situation is described in Jeremiah 34:7.

> The king of Babylon's army fought against Jerusalem and all the cities of Judah that were left, against Lachish and Azekah; for only these fortified cities remained of the cities of Judah.

The Lachish letters were found in the ruins of a guard room at the city gate. Some of the letters were dispatches from an Israelite commander named Hoshaiah to Yaosh, who seems to have been his superior (not all of the letters can be linked clearly to these two men because not all of them contain both names). There is still some dispute whether Hoshaiah was stationed at Lachish or at a nearby outpost. It seems likely, however, that Yaosh was commander at Lachish and Hoshaiah was at a nearby outpost. In Letter IV the writer says:

> And let my lord know that we are watching for the signals of Lachish according to all the indications which my lord hath given, for we cannot see Azekah.

Many have interpreted this as a reference to a time just after the reference in Jeremiah, when Azekah had fallen and only Lachish was left, but the statement is not very specific. Other letters from Lachish include references to "the prophet" and to other names that appear in Jeremiah.

The letters from Arad come from the same period. Most concern the dispensing of provisions, but they also contain references to the house of the Lord and to an apparent encroachment of Edomites.

Other significant ostraca contain a letter complaining of unjust taxation from Yavneh Yam and commodity receipts from Samaria.

Thus pottery speaks through the writing it preserves.

Recording

The recording, which began with the tagging and bagging at excavation, continues when identification numbers are written on important pieces. An important form of recording is the drawing

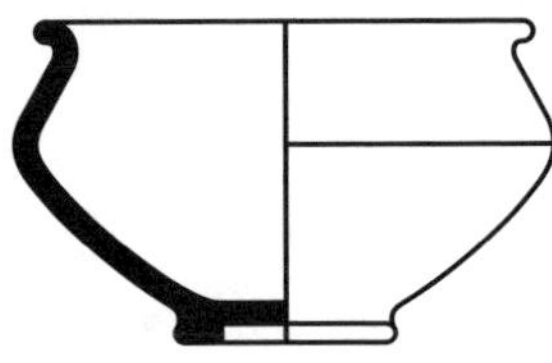

Archaeological Drawing

of the pottery. Whole vessels are drawn in a special style of cutaway drawing. Half of the drawing shows the outside of the vessel with its decoration. The other half is a cutaway that shows the inside of the pot and the profile. Diagnostic sherds are drawn in solid profiles. Computer assisted drawings and databases make these drawings much more readily available for study and research. Such drawings are a major part of site reports and special studies of specific forms of pottery.

Restoration and Display

If enough pieces have survived, the vessel is restored to its former shape by gluing the pieces back together. Remaining holes in the pot are filled in with material that is a slightly different color than the original. This can be a tedious process if there is a lot of pottery of the same size and color that have been jumbled together, as in a looted tomb.

The best or most interesting pieces are displayed in museums. Others are kept for study collections.

Thus pottery has many other values besides its key role in dating sites. For further study: Ruth Amiran, *Ancient Pottery of the Holy Land*, Jerusalem: Massada Press Ltd., 1969.

3

Houses and Cities

Until the 19th century, most of the world's population was comprised of farmers who lived on the land. This was true of ancient Israel. The cities were rather small. They were mainly administrative centers, not centers of production. When David captured Jerusalem, it probably covered only 15-20 acres and had a population of less than five thousand. Though most Israelites were farmers or herders, they did not necessarily live in isolated farmhouses. For security and society, farmers often lived in small villages from which they daily went out to their land.

Houses

The typical house in Israel for much of its history is called the four-room house. This name is a bit misleading, since there may have been more than four rooms and some of the "rooms" were not really rooms. The house basically had four sections. In the middle was a rectangular courtyard, which served as a work area. Entry to the house was through a door at one end of the courtyard. In many cases this courtyard was unroofed. This courtyard was surrounded by "rooms" on three sides. The rooms to the right and left were probably work and storage areas. Sometimes they were set off from the central court by pillars rather than walls, so these areas were more like carports than like rooms. The room or rooms across the back were often the living quarters where the family slept.

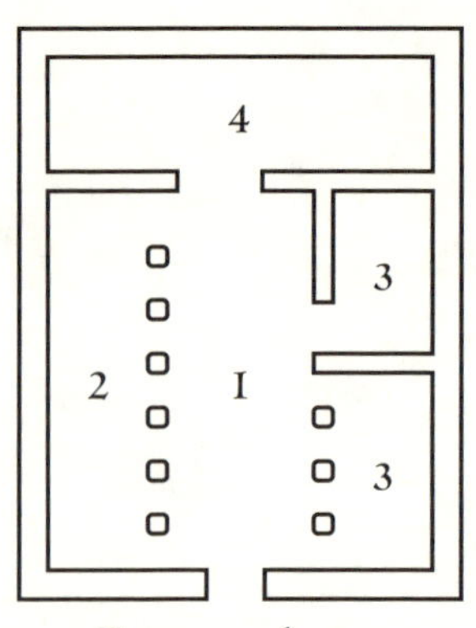
Four-room house

Most areas of the house were multiple-use areas. Bed-rolls were probably folded and stacked during the day. The gear for food preparation and cooking was stored in the side rooms and brought out only when it was to be used. Cooking was probably done in the central courtyard or even outside the house. In this way the smoke of cooking would not be in the house. As there were usually no exterior windows for security reasons, the rooms were probably quite dark and work was done outside whenever possible.

Houses of more well-to-do families may have had a second story that followed the same layout. In such cases the first floor was probably designated for work areas and for the animals and the second story for family living areas. Even in the one-story houses, animals, at least the more valuable ones like donkeys or oxen, probably spent the night in the courtyard. Evidence for this is the presence of mangers in the courtyards.

In both one- and two-story houses, the flat roof was a part of the work area. There are many references to rooftop activities in the Bible.

Deuteronomy 22:8. When you build a new house, make a parapet around your roof so that you may not bring the guilt of bloodshed on your house if someone falls from the roof.

Joshua 2:6. [Rahab] had taken [the spies] up to the roof and hidden them under the stalks of flax she had laid out on the roof.

2 Samuel 11:2. One evening David got up from his bed and walked around on the roof of the palace.

2 Kings 4:9,10. She said to her husband, "I know that this man [Elisha] who often comes our way is a holy man of God. Let's make a small room on the roof and put in it a bed and a table, a chair and a lamp for him. Then he can stay there whenever he comes to us."

Proverbs 21:9. Better to live on a corner of the roof than share a house with a quarrelsome wife.

Mark 13:15. Let no one on the roof of his house go down or enter the house to take anything out.

Acts 10:9. Peter went up on the roof to pray.

From these passages it seems that the main activities done on the roof were processing agricultural products, socializing, relaxing, and sleeping. Crops that needed to be dried in the sun could be spread out on the roof. Since the houses were very close together, neighbors could probably socialize with one another from one rooftop to another—sort of the equivalent of talking over the backyard fence. During the hot summer months in Israel there is no rain, so sleeping on the roof under the stars was a good way to escape the heat and the cramped quarters of the house. Even today in large cities hot weather may send apartment dwellers "Up on the Roof," as the song says.

The home was the center of production in agricultural societies. All the family members worked together in growing, harvesting, and processing the crops. The main crops in Israel were grain for bread, olives for oil, and grapes for wine.

The grain, mostly barley and wheat, was planted in the fall and harvested in spring. The grain had to be cut, stacked, and carried to the threshing floor. The cutting seems to have been done mostly by the men using handheld sickles with stone or metal cutting blades. The women gathered the grain in bundles. At the threshing floor, which did not have to be more than a hard-packed earthen area located on a hill where it could catch the breeze, the grain was separated from the straw and chaff. An ox or donkey dragged a threshing sled, which was sort of like a toboggan with lots of blades sticking through the bottom, over the grain until the kernels of grain were loosened from the straw and chaff. Then when the evening breeze arose, the grain was thrown up in the air with a winnowing fork. The heavier grain fell back to the threshing floor, but the lighter chaff was blown away. The grain was then stored in large storage jars or silos. The silos were not tall buildings like modern silos but underground pits lined with stones and clay. Various passages in Scripture use this process to illustrate God's anger.

> Hosea 13:3. [The unbelievers in Israel] will be like the morning mist, like the early dew that disappears, like chaff swirling from a threshing floor, like smoke escaping through a window.

> Luke 3:17. [Jesus'] winnowing fork is in his hand to clear his threshing floor and to gather the wheat into his barn, but he will burn up the chaff with unquenchable fire.

The grain had to be milled to flour. This could be done with large millstones about 3 or 4 feet wide. A large cylindical lower stone served as a stationary base. A tapered upper stone was rolled around over the lower stone in a circular motion by an ox or donkey that circled the base. It is this type of mill at which Samson had to play the role of the animal. Jesus refers to this type of millstone in his warning to those who lead children away from him.

> Mark 9:42. If anyone causes one of these little ones who believe in me to sin, it would be better for him to be thrown into the sea with a large millstone tied around his neck.

A millstone of this type has been found in Capernaum very near where Jesus spoke these words. A lot of the milling was done in the home in small quantities, using small hand-operated millstones. The lower stone was placed on the floor of the work area, and the operator then knelt next to the millstone and pushed and pulled the upper stone back and forth across the lower stone with both hands (sort of like scrubbing a floor), grinding the grain. The importance of these millstones and an unconventional use for one of them are described in the Bible.

> Deuteronomy 24:6. Do not take a pair of millstones—not even the upper one—as security for a debt, because that would be taking a man's livelihood as security.

> Judges 9:52,53. But as [Abimelech] approached the entrance to the tower to set it on fire, a woman dropped an upper millstone on his head and cracked his skull.

The bread was baked in dome-shaped ovens made of clay. Most of the other cooking was done over an open fire.

The olives provided oil that was used like butter on bread, as fuel for lamps, and for making body lotions and perfumes. The olives were harvested in the fall by being beaten from the tree with sticks. ("When you beat the olives from your trees, do not go over the branches a second time. Leave what remains for the alien, the fatherless and the widow" [Deuteronomy 24:20].) The olives then had to be crushed to a pulp in a mill like the grain mill described above. The oil that could not be extracted by skimming from the pulp had to be squeezed from the pulp in a press. The pulp was placed on a flat lower surface, and a flat pressing plate was pulled down upon it until all the oil was extracted. There are also small olive mills with a little vat carved into the lower stone to catch the oil.

The grapes also were harvested in the fall. The grapes were often allowed to run flat on the ground so they could catch the dew during a rainless summer and retain the water that was poured on them. Since animals could eat the grapes lying on the ground, a wall and watchtower protected the vineyard (see Isaiah chapter 5). A winepress was often constructed on the site. A winepress consisted of three parts: a flat, plastered floor with a rim around it on which the grapes were piled and two plastered pits dug into the ground. When the grapes were trampled by the feet of the treaders, the grape juice ran into the first vat, where the dregs could settle to the bottom. The purer juice ran from the top of the first vat into the second vat through a pipe that connected them. The juice was then bottled out of the second vat. When Gideon was "threshing wheat in a winepress" (Judges 6:11), he was hiding down in one of these pits in the ground where the Midianites would not see him rather than working up on the threshing floor where he should have been.

Though wine was an Israelite staple, they also made beer. But they were not as dependent on it as some of their neighbors. The Bible refers to two types of alcoholic beverages: *yayin*, which was wine made from grapes, and *shekar*, which was everything else. *Shekar* is often translated "strong drink" or "fermented drink" in English versions of the Bible, but it was not likely a distilled product. Rather it was a grain-based alcoholic beverage, that is, beer. That is, it was sort of like beer. It did not contain hops, and some sort of fruit was often thrown into the mix to help with the fermentation. In this respect it was more like fruit-flavored malt liquor than like beer. Those who have tasted beer made from ancient recipes say ancient beer is an acquired taste. Archaeologists have recovered beer recipes from as early as 3000 B.C. Models and pictures from Egypt portray the brewing process. The grain was sometimes first made into dough or bread from which the beer was then made. Ancient beer-drinking paraphernalia have also been recovered. Beer was often poured from strainer vessels or drunk from a common pot through long metal or reed straws in order to keep the drinkers from getting a mouth full of the debris that remained in the beer. Archaeologists can determine whether ancient peoples were predominately wine or beer drinkers from the trace elements that remain in their bones. Beer was included in the offerings presented to the Lord in the temple (Numbers 28:7).

Another important part of the Israelite economy was herding sheep and goats. Some traces of ancient sheepfolds have been found. In the hills of Judea the stables were often caves. Tradition is that the stable in which Jesus was born was a cave. (Olive presses too were sometimes in caves. *Gethsemane* means "oil press," and tradition has it that the place where Jesus and the disciples stayed at Gethsemane was a cave.) A manger is a feeding or watering trough for animals. Jesus' manger was not likely a wooden box; wood was too precious. In the stable of a palace, the manger would have been carved from stone. In a poor stable it would have been made of clay.

Another archaeological remnant from the herding economy is butter churns. Churns could be the skin bottles that were also used as wine bottles. Milk would be put in the bottle, and it would be hung from a frame similar to a tripod or the frame of a baby swing. The bottle would be swung back and forth until the milk became a kind of cheesy butter or buttery cheese. This method is still used today. Churns also could be made of clay. Though the ancient skins have long since perished, examples of the pottery churns have survived.

Mud or Stone

Most houses were made of mud brick. Sun-dried brick was the standard material. Kiln-fired brick was more expensive. Only the most expensive houses and buildings would have been made of stone.

In most cases all that remains of the mud-brick houses are their stone foundations. The bricks have turned back to mud again unless they were baked hard by fire. Such houses were not very sturdy, and the walls were prone to collapse unless they were kept well-plastered.

On the bright side, if your house collapsed, all you needed to do was make new mud bricks and build a new house on the old foundations. The process of making mud bricks is pictured on wall paintings in Egyptian tombs and can still be observed in many parts of the world today. Such mud-brick walls provided very limited security since determined thieves could dig through them. In Ezekiel 12:5 the prophet performs an ironic play foreshadowing the doom of the king of Judah by digging through the wall of his house to make an escape tunnel. This foreshadowed Zedekiah's vain attempt to escape Jerusalem.

We have no surviving palaces of the Israelite kings, but an Israeli archaeologist believes she may be beginning to uncover the remains of David's palace. The rich often had summer homes in the mountains and winter homes in the warmer lowlands. The Bible describes some of these lavish homes.

> Amos 3:15. "I will tear down the winter house along with the summer house; the houses adorned with ivory will be destroyed and the mansions will be demolished," declares the LORD.

As the prophet warned, these houses have long since been destroyed, but some of the ivory carvings that were on the paneled walls and that adorned the furniture have survived. Sadly, many of them were found in Assyria (Iraq) where they were carried away as booty of war.

From New Testament times, ruins of Herod's palaces have been uncovered at Jerusalem, Jericho (his winter home), Caesarea (his Roman-style capital and seaport), and Masada (his wilderness retreat). These provide striking evidence of his wealth and his right to the title Herod the Great.

Towns and Cities

Many Israelites lived in unfortified or semi-fortified villages. In a semi-fortified village, the houses were built in a circle with the back walls of the houses, which had no doors or windows, forming a sort of circular wall—the equivalent of circling the covered wagons in the Old West. Animals could be herded into the middle. This would provide a degree of protection against predators and local rustlers, but not organized attackers.

In general, fortified towns were government administrative centers for controlling the countryside and collecting taxes. One of the best preserved and restored examples is Beersheba. The city was built in a circular form. The city wall consists of a double wall with rooms between the two walls (this style is called a casemate wall). A street circles the city just inside the wall, giving quick access to the wall in time of attack. Important administrative buildings and shrines are near the gate. The streets are more alleys than streets.

The large cities of Israel were not very large, even by the standards of the day. When David captured Jerusalem, it was a city that covered no more than 15 to 20 acres with a population that probably did not exceed three thousand. At the time Solomon added the Temple Mount, the city covered 30 to 40 acres with a population of about five thousand. Near the end of the Old Testament, when Jerusalem was swelled by refugees from the Northern Kingdom, the city reached about 125 acres and 25,000 in population. Jerusalem in Jesus' day covered about 230 acres and had a population of about 40,000. The population of cities, of course, soared in time of war as people swarmed in from the countryside, seeking the protection of the city walls.

Walls and Towers

Aside from the palaces and temples on the acropolis of the city, the distinguishing mark of a city was its fortifications. City walls were usually mud bricks on stone foundations. In some cases the stone part of the wall was much higher than ground level. Some of the best surviving walls are at Arad and the reconstruction at Dan. The fortifications at Dan are especially interesting because they include a mud-brick archway that was built in the second millennium B.C., evidence that the arch was used much earlier than previously thought. All of the city walls surrounding the Old City of Jerusalem today are from more recent times.

Along the walls, at regular intervals, strong towers project out from the walls, allowing defenders on the walls to rake attackers with crossfire from three directions. The bases of some of the towers that defended Herod's citadel in Jerusalem still survive.

Of special interest are the city gates, or more precisely, the gate structures. The gates were not just big doors into the city; they were often located in a fortified position. Access to the gates was not direct. Often there was a baffle wall blocking direct access to the gate. Those attacking the gate had to go along a ramp parallel to the city wall in order to reach the gate. This made it necessary for them to run a gauntlet of fire from the wall before they even reached the gate. Sometimes there was a double gateway, so if they broke

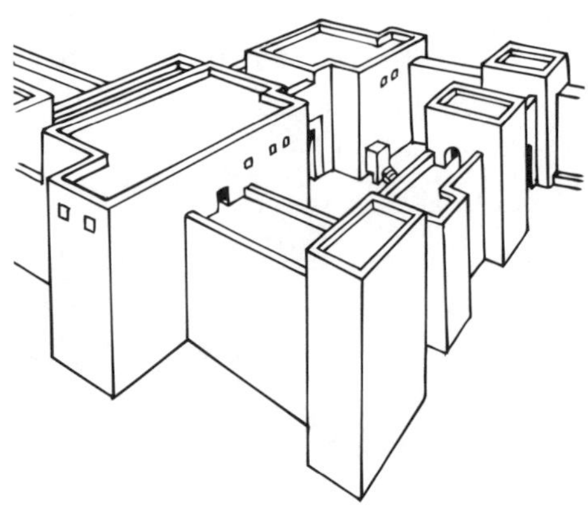

City wall and gate structure

through the first gate, they found themselves in a courtyard where they could be peppered with fire from four sides before they reached the second gate. Once they made it inside the gatehouse, they had to get through a passageway that had three guard rooms on each side where defenders awaited them. Openings in the ceiling probably allowed defenders to also attack them from above.

For all these reasons, cities were seldom captured through the gates, unless the gates were opened by traitors. To capture the city, attackers had to breech the city wall with battering rams. Since the city walls were usually located at the top of a high mound, the first step was to build an earthen ramp to the base or top of the wall. This was often done by captured prisoners of war. If the defenders killed the workers with fire from the wall, they were killing their own people. Once the wall was reached by the ramp, towers and battering rams could be wheeled up the ramp to the wall. We have pictures of such machines operating against the Judean city of Lachish in Sennacherib's memorial murals of the attack. The defenders could try to thwart the battering rams by tearing down houses and piling them against the wall at the point of attack. Another tactic was to dig a tunnel under the ramp from inside the city in the hopes of collapsing the ramp.

Two of the best examples of surviving siege ramps in Israel are the Assyrian ramp against Lachish and the huge Roman ramp against Masada. Examples of undermining tunnels have been found in surrounding countries.

Attackers also often built their own walls and trenches all the way around the city to prevent any escapes from the city and to prevent reinforcements from reaching the city. Traces of such walls exist at Gath and Masada. At Masada one can also see the outlines of the Roman camps that surrounded the besieged stronghold.

When the city was captured, the consequences were terrible. Many of the people were enslaved and deported. Leaders were tortured by having parts of their body cut off, being skinned alive, and finally being impaled on poles. Pyramids were built out of the heads of the executed leaders. All of these atrocities are pictured on the Assyrian memorials of their campaigns.

The City Gate

The gatehouse served an important social function in times of peace. Markets and shrines were located by the gate. The courtyards by the gate or the rooms within the gatehouse served as meeting places where parties met to sign contracts or resolve legal disputes. The gates were a high-traffic area—a great place to make announcements. The city gate was also a reception area for the king, where he met his subjects or reviewed his troops. Criminals were executed at the city gate. There are many references to this function of the city gate in the Bible. In some respects the city gate was the most important spot in the city.

The city gate was the public center of the city and the meeting place for the elders of the city. There justice was dispensed, and honor and rebuke were distributed.

Proverbs 31:23,31. Her husband is respected at the city gate, where he takes his seat among the elders of the land. Give her the reward she has earned, and let her works bring her praise at the city gate.

Lamentations 5:14. The elders are gone from the city gate; the young men have stopped their music.

Joshua 20:4. When [the fugitive] flees to one of these cities [of refuge], he is to stand in the entrance of the city gate and state his case before the elders of that city.

Ruth 4:1. Boaz went up to the town gate and sat there. When the kinsman-redeemer he had mentioned came along, Boaz said, "Come over here, my friend, and sit down." [Boaz then made the arrangements to marry Ruth and redeem Naomi's land.]

Shrines were built at the gates.

2 Kings 23:8. Josiah brought all the priests from the towns of Judah and desecrated the high places, from Geba to Beersheba, where the priests had burned incense. He broke down the shrines at the gates—at the entrance to the Gate of Joshua, the city governor, which is on the left of the city gate.

The gate served as a royal reception area.

1 Kings 22:10. Dressed in their royal robes, the king of Israel and Jehoshaphat king of Judah were sitting on their thrones at the threshing floor by the entrance of the gate of Samaria, with all the prophets prophesying before them.

2 Chronicles 32:6. [The king] appointed military officers over the people and assembled them before him in the square at the city gate and encouraged them with these words.

Such a royal reception area, including the throne platform, has been restored in the city gate area of Dan. The city gate played a key role in the tragedy of David and Absalom.

2 Samuel 15:2. [Absalom] would get up early and stand by the side of the road leading to the city gate. Whenever anyone came with a complaint to be placed before the king for

a decision, Absalom would call out to him, "What town are you from?"

2 Samuel 18:24. While David was sitting between the inner and outer gates [waiting for news about Absalom], the watchman went up to the roof of the gateway by the wall. As he looked out, he saw a man running alone.

2 Samuel 19:8. So the king got up and took his seat in the gateway. When the men were told, "The king is sitting in the gateway," they all came before him.

The gate served as the place of execution.

Deuteronomy 17:5. Take the man or woman who has done this evil deed to your city gate and stone that person to death.

Joshua 8:29. He hung the king of Ai on a tree and left him there until evening. At sunset, Joshua ordered them to take his body from the tree and throw it down at the entrance of the city gate. And they raised a large pile of rocks over it, which remains to this day.

2 Kings 10:8. When the messenger arrived, he told Jehu, "They have brought the heads of the princes." Then Jehu ordered, "Put them in two piles at the entrance of the city gate until morning."

Hebrews 13:12. Jesus also suffered outside the city gate to make the people holy through his own blood.

The Temple Gates

The temple gates, which were constructed in the same manner as the city gates, also served the same kind of function as a meeting place.

Acts 3:1,2. One day Peter and John were going up to the temple at the time of prayer—at three in the afternoon. Now a man crippled from birth was being carried to the temple gate called Beautiful, where he was put every day to beg from those going into the temple courts.

Posting news at the gate was the equivalent to Luther's nailing the Ninety-five Theses to the door of the Castle Church in Wittenberg.

Jeremiah 7:2. Stand at the gate of the LORD's house and there proclaim this message.

There is an elaborate description of the architecture and use of the gatehouses in Ezekiel's closing vision of the new temple. The gatehouse was where the action was.

4

Water Systems

Water is essential to life, but water is not the source from which life emerged, as evolutionists claim. God brought both animal and human life from the ground, not from the water. But just as water is essential to bring plant life from the ground, water is the most essential element for sustaining human life on the earth. Plants, animals, and humans can't live without water.

The value of water was especially clear to the Israelites, who lived in a water-challenged environment. Civilizations grew up in the great river valleys of the world—the Nile in Egypt, the Tigris and Euphrates in Mesopotamia (the land between the rivers), the Indus in India, and the Yellow River in China. Israel, however, has no major river. Even the Jordan is barely big enough to be called a river.

A further challenge is that the rains in Israel are very seasonal. The "early rains" in October get the grain started. Most of the rain falls in midwinter, in January and February. The "latter rains" in March and April are needed to ready the grain for harvest. From May to September there is virtually no rain.

Unlike the irrigation-based societies of Egypt and Mesopotamia, Israel was dependent on getting rain at just the right time. None of the rivers in Israel were suitable for irrigation with ancient technology. A small deficit in the early or latter rains meant disaster. Israel's environment taught them to depend on the Lord for rain in its season. In Deuteronomy chapter 11:11-17 God promised Israel:

> The land you are crossing the Jordan to take possession of is a land of mountains and valleys that drinks rain from heaven. It is a land the LORD your God cares for; the eyes of the LORD your God are continually on it from the beginning of the year to its end. So if you faithfully obey the commands I am giving you today—to love the LORD your God and to serve him with all your heart and with all your soul—then I will send rain on your land in its season, both autumn and spring rains, so that you may gather in your

grain, new wine and oil. I will provide grass in the fields for your cattle, and you will eat and be satisfied. Be careful, or you will be enticed to turn away and worship other gods and bow down to them. Then the LORD's anger will burn against you, and he will shut the heavens so that it will not rain and the ground will yield no produce, and you will soon perish from the good land the LORD is giving you.

Much of Israel's tragic history revolves around the quest for water. All too often they turned to the *baals,* the rain gods, for help. The result was that the Lord withheld rain until the Israelites returned to him. Water was a matter of life or death, both physically and spiritually.

In the Bible, water, which is the sustainer of earthly life, is also the symbol of God's Word, which sustains spiritual life—the life that is eternal. To the Samaritan woman who came to draw water from the well of Jacob, Jesus said:

> John 4:13,14. "Everyone who drinks this water will be thirsty again, but whoever drinks the water I give him will never thirst. Indeed, the water I give him will become in him a spring of water welling up to eternal life."

The rivers of Eden are "types" of the river of life that appears in the city of God in Psalm 46, that flows from Jerusalem in Ezekiel's vision in Ezekiel chapter 47, and that waters the New Jerusalem in Revelation chapter 22.

The urgent search for water that characterized the history of Israel is a constant reminder of the need for the water of eternal life.

> Psalm 1:3. [The righteous man] is like a tree planted by streams of water, which yields its fruit in season and whose leaf does not wither.

Sources of Water

LIVING WATER

Living water is water from a stream or spring. When the population is small, the sources of water are very simple: go to the stream or spring, and take the water you need.

SPRINGS

Since there are relatively few streams in Israel that flow year-round, life in early Israel centered around the springs.

Psalm 104:10-12. [The Lord] makes springs pour water into the ravines; it flows between the mountains. They give water to all the beasts of the field; the wild donkeys quench their thirst. The birds of the air nest by the waters; they sing among the branches.

Many place names in Israel contain *En*, the Hebrew word for "spring." The locations of springs dictated the locations of settlements.

WELLS

When the springs dry up, men must dig down to the water table below. Simple, hand-dug wells were the first man-made water sources in Israel. These wells are not narrow pipes like our modern wells but pits dug into the ground. Some of them are 15 or 20 feet wide and are lined with stone walls.

In certain regions of the country, especially in the dry Negev in the south, wells are rare and precious and, therefore, a source of strife and contention. The lives of Abraham and Isaac were punctuated by contention with their neighbors over the wells that they needed for their herds (Genesis chapters 21 and 26). Many place names in Israel contain the Hebrew for "well," which is *Beer*—most famously, Beersheba, "the well of the oath" or "the well of seven."

Pools and Cisterns

There had to be a method of saving the plentiful winter rain for summer use. Rainwater could be collected in open pools or in closed underground cisterns. Modern cisterns are usually metal or concrete tanks for collecting rainwater. Ancient cisterns were pits or "rooms" dug out of the rock to collect the rainwater. The fact that they were closed at the top, except for a narrow opening to pour in and to draw out water, minimized evaporation. At first cisterns were not very effective since the water seeped away through the porous rock. When the art of lining the cisterns with lime plaster was developed around

1000 B.C., cisterns became an effective method of supporting urban populations larger than those that could be supported by the limited output of springs. Some cisterns are small chambers under private homes. Others are huge underground rooms, 30 feet high and 100 feet long. The whole area under the Temple Mount in Jerusalem is honeycombed with large underground cisterns that are capable of holding millions of gallons of water. The cisterns at the base of Herod's desert fortress of Masada held more than ten million gallons of water.

Cisterns play into Bible history in two ways: as water sources and as prisons or dumps.

According to tradition, Jesus was held in a cistern under Caiphas' palace. Joseph (Genesis chapter 37) and Jeremiah (Jeremiah chapter 38) were both imprisoned in cisterns.

Jeremiah 38:6-13. So they took Jeremiah and put him into the cistern of Malkijah, the king's son, which was in the courtyard of the guard. They lowered Jeremiah by ropes into the cistern; it had no water in it, only mud, and Jeremiah sank down into the mud. But Ebed-Melech, a Cushite, an official in the royal palace, heard that they had put Jeremiah into the cistern. While the king was sitting in the Benjamin Gate, Ebed-Melech went out of the palace and said to him, "My lord the king, these men have acted wickedly in all they have done to Jeremiah the prophet. They have thrown him into a cistern, where he will starve to death when there is no longer any bread in the city." Then the king commanded Ebed-Melech the Cushite, "Take thirty men from here with you and lift Jeremiah the prophet out of the cistern before he dies." So Ebed-Melech took the men with him and went to a room under the treasury in the palace. He took some old rags and worn-out clothes from there and let them down with ropes to Jeremiah in the cistern. Ebed-Melech the Cushite said to Jeremiah, "Put these old rags and worn-out clothes under your arms to pad the ropes." Jeremiah did so, and they pulled him up with the ropes and lifted him out of the cistern. And Jeremiah remained in the courtyard of the guard.

In Jeremiah chapter 41 a cistern was used as a mass grave for the victims of a massacre.

People probably preferred the fresh, living water of springs and streams, but in Israel's climate cisterns were a necessity. Without them larger concentrations of population would not have been possible.

Elaborate Systems

Even with the development of cisterns, the springs remained important. The problem was that the cities were often on the top of a high hill and the springs were at the base of the hill. In peacetime this was an inconvenience, but not a problem. Inhabitants could just go down the hill, get the water, and carry it back up. Wartime created a double problem: how to prevent the besiegers from getting the water and how to get the water into the city. To solve this problem, elaborate water systems were created.

There were three basic solutions to the problem: (1) in the center of the city dig a large open-pit well down to the water table (these shafts could double as an open-topped cistern to collect rain water); (2) dig a closed tunnel down to the water table beneath the city; or (3) dig a tunnel to the spring that lay outside the city walls. The most complex systems combined these methods.

The following three systems illustrate each type, though all of them combine both vertical shafts and tunnels.

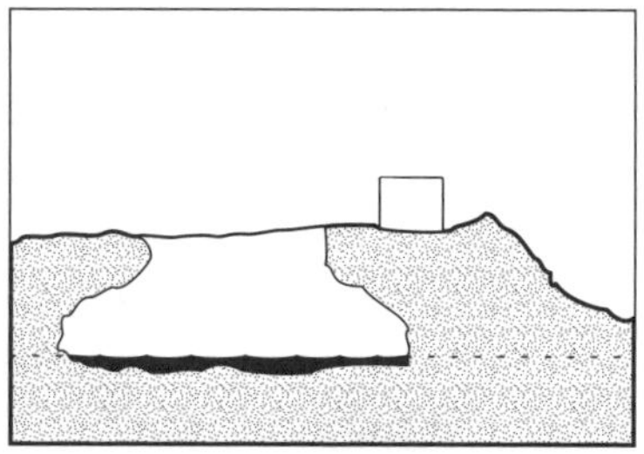

Open-Pit Well

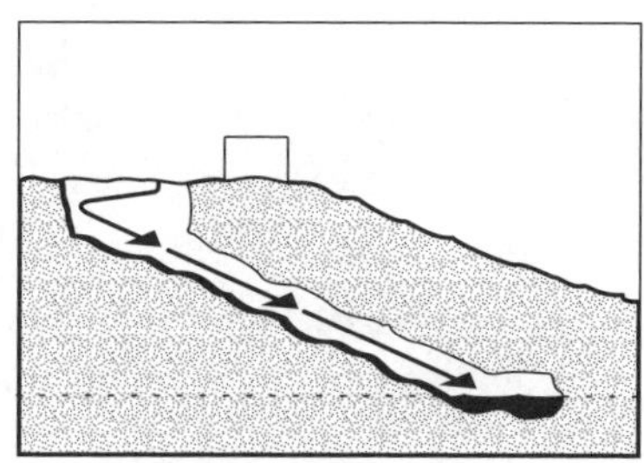

Tunnel to Water Table

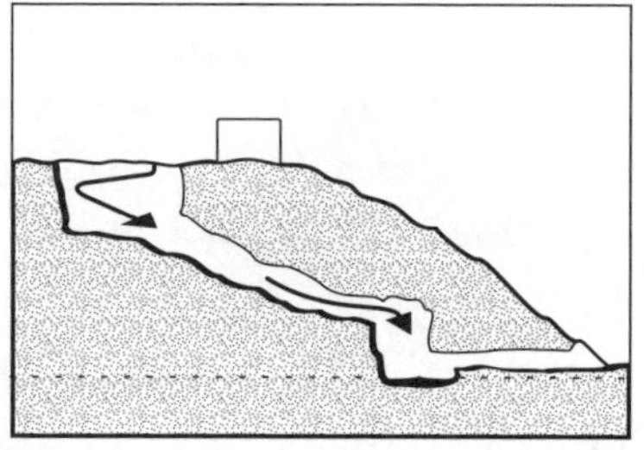

Tunnel to the Spring

THE POOL OF GIBEON

The first stage of the great pool at Gibeon is an example of a big-pit well. The well's first stage, the "big pit," is a round shaft, 37 feet wide, cut down through the limestone to a depth of 35 feet. A spiral staircase encircles this shaft to its bottom. The second stage of the system is a narrower tunnel with steps that allow water carriers to descend to a water-drawing room 82 feet below the surface to draw ground water. This system seems to be the same system that the Bible calls a pool. Some have suggested that this name derives from the fact that rainwater was collected into the shaft during the rainy season. During high water periods, users had to go only partway down the steps to draw water. By the end of the dry season, they had to descend to ground water through the tunnel.

Two battles took place near this pool. The first was the battle between David's men led by Joab and Ish-Bosheth's men led by Abner (2 Samuel chapter 2), and the second was Johanan's rescue of the hostages from Ishmael in Jeremiah chapter 41.

THE HAZOR TUNNEL

The water system at Hazor, probably built during the time of Ahab, was a tunnel to the water table inside the city wall. The system at Hazor began as a rectangular shaft about 50 feet wide, dug to a depth of over 60 feet. A winding staircase of stone steps along the walls led to the bottom. From the bottom of the shaft, a tunnel 15 feet wide and 15 feet high sloped down in a series of steps for more than 90 feet until it reached the water table. A modern staircase of 150 steps laid over the original steps enables modern visitors to reach the water basin at the bottom.

THE MEGIDDO TUNNEL

The similar system at Megiddo reached a spring outside the city walls. The water system began with a square 80-foot-deep vertical shaft and a 250-foot-long horizontal tunnel. In order to hide the source of water from the enemy and to protect the users of the water system, a thick wall, camouflaged by a covering of earth, was constructed at the entrance to the cave from which the spring flows, blocking access from the outside.

The Water System of Jerusalem From Old Testament Times

The water system of Jerusalem is the most complex and most important water system of ancient Israel. It was actually two water systems: the original tunnel complex and the later addition of Hezekiah's Tunnel.

The water supply for Jerusalem was the Gihon Spring, which lies at the bottom of the eastern side of the lower southeast hill of Jerusalem, now known as the City of David. Much higher hills lie to the north (the Temple Mount) and to the west (today's Mount Zion), but the city could not be built on these more defensible hills until cisterns and aqueducts were developed. Three water systems were connected to the Gihon Spring.

THE SILOAM CHANNEL

In peacetime the water could be directed southward through the Kidron Valley, where it could be used to water gardens and orchards. The Siloam Channel, cut at the beginning of the second millennium B.C., starts from the Gihon Spring and runs approximately 1,200 feet southward along the eastern slope of the City of David, around the city's southern end, and into a reservoir in the central valley of Jerusalem. The channel's northern part is 9 feet deep and is covered by large stones. The southern part is open but becomes a rock-cut tunnel near the end. Openings along the channel allowed water to flow out and irrigate the terraces on the eastern slope of the City of David. Some identify the Siloam Channel with "the gently flowing waters of Shiloah" (Isaiah 8:6). After the cutting of Hezekiah's Tunnel, this channel was blocked. This effort to prevent enemy access to the water may be referred to in 2 Chronicles 32:4, which says, "A large force of men assembled, and they blocked all the springs and the stream that flowed through the land. 'Why should the kings of Assyria come and find plenty of water?' they said."

WARREN'S SHAFT

During times of war, the water had to be accessed by a tunnel from within the city. The first system constructed to do this is now known as Warren's Shaft, in honor of the explorer who rediscovered it in 1867. It was cleared and reopened during excavations in the 1980s. The upper entrance to the Warren's Shaft system is located in the middle of the eastern slope of the City of David, within the ancient city's walls. It consists of a rock-cut tunnel with a vertical shaft at its lower end. From the upper entrance, the tunnel slopes steeply downward in a stepped passage. This portion is covered by a well-constructed vault from the Second Temple (New Testament) Period, which prevented soil and rocks from falling into the system. Farther down, the tunnel becomes less steep. At first it extends in a northeasterly direction, then it angles sharply to the southeast. The total length of the tunnel is about 125 feet, and it descends about 40 feet. Its width is 7 to 10 feet, and its height varies from 4 feet at the entrance to a maximum of 15 feet. At its end, one comes to a narrow, irregularly shaped vertical shaft about 3-5 feet wide and 40 feet deep. Waters from the Gihon Spring collect at the bottom, and it is possible to draw them up by dropping a bucket down the shaft.

After the discovery of Warren's Shaft, some Bible students proposed that this shaft could be identified with the *tsinnor* (Hebrew, "pipe" or "shaft") mentioned in the Bible as the means by which Joab gained access to the city in order to capture it for David. David said, "Anyone who conquers the Jebusites will have to use the water shaft to reach those 'lame and blind' who are David's enemies" (2 Samuel 5:8). First Chronicles chapter 11 says that Joab led the ascent into the city, but it makes no mention of the shaft.

The understanding of this system was changed dramatically by new discoveries in the 1990s. Excavations next to the Gihon Spring uncovered remains of two massive towers of enormous stones that protruded eastward from the line of the city wall. Between them was a deep rock-cut pool. The towers protected the spring and the pool, denying access to them while guaranteeing the water supply in time of siege. The excavators dated this fortification system to the beginning of the second millennium B.C., long before David's conquest of the city. A short section of the upper tunnel extending eastward from the vertical shaft was cleared and found to lead toward the pool and towers just described. This suggests that both the upper tunnel and lower pool and the fortifications were part of one system and that the vertical shaft was not needed to access the water. This led to the proposal that the vertical shaft was not part of the original system but was a natural cave discovered accidentally when the floor of the upper tunnel was lowered, perhaps in the eighth century B.C. The relationship of this system to David's *tsinnor* is currently the subject of debate.

HEZEKIAH'S TUNNEL

Hezekiah's Tunnel is the last and most impressive of the water systems built for the City of David. Although its existence was known for hundreds of years, its systematic investigation was undertaken only in the 19th century. Thorough study and mapping were carried out by H. Vincent between 1909 and 1911.

The purpose of the tunnel was to carry the water from the Gihon Spring under the City of David and into the central valley of Jerusalem, which was now protected by an extension of the city wall. The tunnel was cut into the rock beneath the City of David by miners digging from both ends. It follows an *S*-shaped course about 1,700 feet long. Its outlet is the Pool of Siloam. In a straight line, the distance from the Gihon Spring to the Siloam Pool is only a thousand feet. Why did the miners follow such a long course, especially since they were in a hurry to be ready for the impending Assyrian invasion? It is easier to dig a straight-line tunnel to a meeting point than a curvy one (all the miners had to do was look backward to daylight and to posts in a line outside the mouth of the tunnel). An examination of the tunnel makes it clear that the miners were for the most part following natural caves through the soft limestone. The average width of the tunnel is about 2-3 feet. It is about 6 feet high along most of its course, but reaches 10-15 feet high in some sections near the beginning and the end. It is very easy to distinguish the parts that are natural caves from the parts carved by the miners. The carved parts are just the right size and height for a miner. The high parts are clearly natural caves. Once the caves had been connected, the miners had to level the floor so the water would run through. The midpoint meeting of the two crews that completed the tunnel is described in a six-line inscription, written in the old Hebrew alphabet, which the workmen inscribed in the wall of the tunnel. It says:

. . . breakthrough and this was the account of the break-through. While the laborers were still working with their picks, each toward the other, and while there were still three cubits to be broken through, the voice of each was heard calling to the other, because there was a *zdh* [crack?] in the rock to the south and to the north. And at the moment of the breakthrough, the laborers struck each toward the other, pick against pick. Then the water flowed from the spring to the pool for 1,200 cubits. And the height of the rock above the heads of the laborers was 100 cubits.

This inscription, known as the Siloam Inscription, discovered at the end of the 19th century, was removed from the tunnel and is now in the Archaeological Museum of Istanbul. (Palestine was under Turkish rule at the time.)

This project is mentioned in the Bible in 2 Kings 20:20: "As for the other events of Hezekiah's reign, all his achievements and how he made the pool and the tunnel by which he brought water into the city, are they not written in the book of the annals of the kings of Judah?" It is mentioned again in 2 Chronicles 32:30: "It was Hezekiah who blocked the upper outlet of the Gihon Spring and channeled the water down to the west side of the City of David. He succeeded in everything he undertook."

Since the removal of the debris that blocked Warren's Shaft, the tunnel has been open to visitors. At the end of the tunnel, one can look down the natural shaft. From the cave of the Gihon Spring, one can also look up the vertical shaft from below. Visitors can also wade through Hezekiah's Tunnel by candlelight or flashlight. The water varies from hip deep to shin deep. The trip is one of the highlights of a visit to Jerusalem.

New Testament Water Systems

Cisterns and pools to collect rainwater remained important parts of the New Testament water systems. Two of these pools are of special interest.

THE POOL OF BETHESDA

We should actually say the *pools* of Bethesda, since Bethesda was two large pools separated by a rock partition that stood between them. The twin pools were surrounded by porticos on four sides. A fifth portico was on the partition. The twin pools are located just north of the Temple Mount in the northeast quarter of the city. Some think this location may be the same as that of the Upper Pool mentioned in the Old Testament in 2 Kings 18:17: "The king of Assyria sent his supreme commander, his chief officer and his field commander with a large army, from Lachish to King Hezekiah at Jerusalem. They came up to Jerusalem and stopped at the aqueduct of the Upper Pool, on the road to the Washerman's Field." However, the reference to the Washerman's Field suggests that the Upper Pool may have been in the valley. The general location of Bethesda seems to be identical with or perhaps close to the Sheep Pool, where sacrificial animals for the temple were washed.

This pool was the site of Jesus' healing of the crippled man in John chapter 5. In addition to collecting rainwater, these pools were spring fed. This may account for the "stirring of the waters," which was attributed to angelic presence by those who came to the pools to be healed. This stirring may also have been caused by the passage of water through a conduit between the pools. (The reference to this stirring in John chapter 5 may not be part of the original text.)

The pools might more aptly be called reservoirs than pools. The two pools are about 160 feet by 200 feet and 135 feet by 175 feet. The pools are about 30 feet deep. The partition between the pools is 20 feet wide. It is understandable why the lame man needed help. At high water, the water was up to 30 feet deep. At low water, one had to go down many steps to reach it.

The meaning of the name of the pool is much disputed, and several variants occur in the biblical text. It is often interpreted as "House of Mercy," but the name may be short for *Beth Eshdathayin,* "House of the Twin Pools."

THE POOL OF SILOAM

Today the Pool of Siloam, at the southern outlet of Hezekiah's Tunnel, is a small shallow pool (50 feet by 15 feet). In New Testament times, the Pool of Siloam was surrounded by a colonnaded porch 75 feet square.

The identification of this pool with Siloam is complicated by the discovery of another pool somewhat further down the valley. A pool in this lower area could receive not only the water from Gihon but also runoff from the central valley during the rainy season. This area seems to have been outside the city wall, where Josephus places Siloam. In 2004 workers repairing a sewer in the suspected location of the lower pool uncovered stone steps. It quickly became clear that these steps had been part of a Second Temple (New Testament) Period pool. This pool is less than one hundred yards from the upper pool.

The bottom of the pool is reached by three flights of five steps each, separated by landings. It has been suggested that the steps were designed to accommodate various water levels. The pool is stone lined, but underneath there is evidence of an earlier version that was merely plastered. Coins found within this plaster date from the time of the Hasmonean king Alexander Jannaeus (104–76 B.C.). The pool, which is only partly excavated, has been estimated to be 225 feet long. It is much shallower than Bethesda.

A channel leads from the upper pool, which must have originated in the time of Hezekiah, to feed this later, lower pool. It is debatable which of these pools was Jesus' Siloam, where he healed the man born blind (John chapter 9). This lower Siloam pool is probably the Lower Pool of Hezekiah's day.

It is understandable why Jesus conducted part of his ministry at these pools. Such pools were important social centers where one could expect to find crowds of people.

Aqueducts

A new element of New Testament water systems was aqueducts to bring in water from nearby mountains. *Aqueduct* may refer to any man-made water channel, but we associate the term with the high aqueducts of the Roman period that carried water over long distances. Most of the aqueducts in Israel are much lower than the towering aqueducts nearly 150 feet high that are found in some areas of the Roman Empire. Tunnels and bridges are means to adjust the route of an aqueduct to the specific terrain. Ancient aqueducts operated by gravity flow, so the engineers normally followed the natural contours around hills and mountains. This meant constructing long, circuitous routes, but this was in most cases cheaper than the alternatives: boring tunnels through mountains and hills, and constructing bridges, arcades, or inverted siphons across valleys.

Inverted siphons were the most interesting features of ancient aqueducts. Where valleys were too broad or too deep and where a detour was impractical, one solution was a siphon. Already in the second millennium B.C., engineers in Crete had discovered that water in a *U*-shaped tube rises to the same level in both legs—the "law of communicating vessels." If water from an open channel is run into an airtight pipe at the top of a hill on one side of a valley, it will descend to the bottom of the valley and climb back up the other side of the valley to almost the original level, where it can again flow into an open conduit to continue its journey. This technique was used in aqueducts in Israel, including the Jerusalem temple aqueduct.

At the time of Jesus, aqueducts carried water from the higher hills south of Bethlehem to the Temple Mount, entering the temple on a bridge that crossed the central valley. Pilate seems to have played a role in the construction, repair, or completion of one of these aqueducts (the project probably originated with Herod the Great). Rather than gaining favor for Pilate, this project set off a riot because Pilate had used money from the temple treasury to pay for it. The death of Jewish protestors at the hands of Pilate's bodyguards was one of the black marks against Pilate's administration that eventually led to his dismissal.

At least two aqueducts carried water from the so-called Pools of Solomon, about 10 miles south of Jerusalem. The lower-level aqueduct traces the winding contours of the Judean hills for a distance of about 15 miles before reaching the "Great Sea," a cistern under the Temple Mount. Its date is uncertain, but it may be Herodian. The course of another aqueduct, known as the high-level aqueduct, is only partially known.

The best-known aqueducts in Israel are the twin aqueducts servicing Herod's port of Caesarea with water carried from Mount Carmel. One of these aqueducts, built by Herod, carried water 6 miles from Mount Carmel in a single channel. Near the city this aqueduct is carried on arches, but they are not particularly high. The little "rooms" under the arches make nice shady pavilions if you happen to be fortunate enough to be on the beach north of Caesarea. A northern extension of this aqueduct runs in underground tunnels below Mount Carmel. These tunnels seem to be post-Herodian, as is the second channel added to the original aqueduct. The third channel of the first aqueduct and the second aqueduct that runs parallel to the first are from much later.

Baths

Among the Jews, *baths* were the hot-tub-sized pools known as *mikvehs* used for ceremonial cleansing. Ritual washings in order to be cleansed from ceremonial uncleanness were prescribed in the Old Testament law, but by the time of Christ, a very elaborate set of rules governing the construction and use of these baths had been developed.

Such baths are found at many sites in Israel, including more than 150 in Jerusalem. Such a bath would have been used by Mary in her purification after Jesus' birth.

Some have seen a connection between these baths and Baptism. In a certain sense the Old Testament washings are a predecessor or type of Baptism, but they are quite different in purpose. Washing in a *mikveh* was a repeated act that cleansed from ceremonial pollution. Baptism is a one-time event for forgiveness of sins.

The second type of bath found in Israel was the Roman and Greek-style public bathhouse. These baths were like a spa or health club that also served as a social club. Roman baths were elaborate structures with a variety of hot and cold baths. The Roman baths at Hamat Gadar, which make use of natural hot springs, are especially well preserved. This bath complex near the eastern shore of the Sea of Galilee was constructed after the time of Jesus. Such baths were used by those Jews who were assimilating to Roman and Greek culture but were not likely frequented by Jesus and his disciples.

Christians living in the Greek cities, however, did frequent the baths. The church father Ireneus reports that the apostle John once rushed out of the bathhouse in which he was bathing when he realized that the arch-heretic Cerinthus was also bathing there. John would practice no bath fellowship with heretics.

At his various estates, Herod, a man who tried to have one foot in each of two worlds, had both Jewish *mikvehs* and Roman-style bathhouses, as well as swimming pools. Herod's three winter palaces at the warm oasis of Jericho had the epitome of a luxurious water system. Aqueducts brought water for the palace gardens. There were a number of swimming pools. One of the elaborate bathhouses had several rooms decorated with frescos. The main room in the bathhouse had a mosaic floor with red, black, and white geometric patterns. The bathhouses included hot and cold baths as well as *mikvehs*. The hot room was heated by hot air that circulated under the floor, warming it. But even in his high-class baths, Herod was still Herod, a low-class killer. The historian Josephus reports that a young Hasmonean in-law of Herod's, whom Herod feared was a threat to his throne, was "accidentally" drowned in Herod's pool by the "lifeguards" who were roughhousing with him. The lifestyle of the rich and famous was not without its hazards.

Toilets and Sewers

Deuteronomy 23:12-14 specifies that for the Israelites in the wilderness, their toilets, which were just shallow holes in the ground, were to be outside the camp, and the waste was to be covered with earth. This was not primarily for hygiene but for ceremonial cleanness. These regulations posed some practical problems for strictly observant Israelites like the Essenes if they lived in larger communities like Jerusalem. Their latrines had to be outside the city in roofed "outhouses" so that no human waste could be seen in or near the city. Since the strictest among them believed that they could not leave the city on the Sabbath, this practice likely posed a problem at times.

Also at Qumran, a community that is most connected with the Essenses, a latrine area has been found a considerable distance outside the community.

Many other Israelites were less scrupulous, and the well-to-do had indoor toilets in their homes in Jerusalem. Some indoor toilets were just a chair with a hole in it, under which a chamber pot could be placed, but a number of stone toilet seats have been found from the destruction layer of Old Testament Jerusalem. Indoor flush toilets (using a pot of water to flush the pipes) are at least four thousand years old, but little is known of the system in Jerusalem. Waste was probably disposed outside the city.

The Roman world also had large public "restrooms" with many toilets in a row. There were no stalls separating the toilets and no toilet paper. Users wiped themselves with a sponge on a stick that was wetted with water from a trough that ran in front of the toilet. A famous example is found in the city of Ephesus, but an example also exists in Israel in Beth Shan, which was a gentile city. This lavatory with 40 seats was for patrons of other nearby public facilities. Water from a large tank flowed into a deep channel beneath the seats to wash away waste. Young boys, we are told, were hired to sit on the cold stone seats to warm them up for the well-to-do clientele.

Archaeologists are interested not so much in the toilets themselves but in the soil that is under them. Though it is now fairly harmless, regular-looking soil, it preserves evidence of the parasites and the diet that passed through the ancient users.

Clay sewer pipes are found at many sites. Cities had sewer systems of sorts and faced the same problem that plagues modern cities: keeping wastewater separate from storm water, which was collected in cisterns for drinking. The sewers of Herod's Caesarea were designed to be flushed by the sea.

Archaeologists have recently uncovered a large sewer that runs down the central valley of Jerusalem. During the destruction of Jerusalem in A.D. 70, it was used as a hiding place and possibly an escape tunnel by inhabitants fleeing the Roman onslaught.

The Bible may record another unpleasant escape in Judges 3:20-26—the account of the assassination of Eglon, the king of Moab, by the judge Ehud.

> Ehud then approached [Eglon] while he was sitting alone in the upper room of his summer palace and said, "I have a message from God for you." As the king rose from his seat, Ehud reached with his left hand, drew the sword from his right thigh and plunged it into the king's belly. Even the handle sank in after the blade, which came out his back. Ehud did not pull the sword out, and the fat closed in over it. Then Ehud went out to the porch; he shut the doors of the upper room behind him and locked them. After he had gone, the servants came and found the doors of the upper room locked. They said, "He must be relieving himself in the inner room of the house." They waited to the point of embarrassment, but when he did not open the doors of the room, they took a key and unlocked them. There they saw their lord fallen to the floor, dead. While they waited, Ehud got away.

The notes in the NIV say that the meaning of the words translated "upper room" and "porch" are uncertain. The view of the NIV seems to be that Ehud simply left the suite and locked the doors behind him, without the guards seeing him do it. Another view is that Ehud escaped the upper room, which he had locked from the inside, by jumping off the balcony. The third view is that Ehud jumped down into the pit of the suite's indoor toilet and escaped through the place where the toilet was emptied. Whether the porch or the toilet was Ehud's escape route, the text shows clearly that palaces of the second millennium B.C. had indoor toilets even in the upper story.

The water systems and plumbing of the ancient world were more sophisticated than we might think, and Israel shared in this progress.

Israel was unique in the ancient world in that only there had the Lord preserved the knowledge that he is the only God. He had brought Abraham away from the idolatry of his father, Terah, in Ur and Haran. He led Abraham to a new land. He made his covenant with the patriarchs and brought their descendants up out of Egypt. At Sinai he made a covenant with Israel. He gave the Israelites the tabernacle as the one place of worship where they were to offer sacrifices to him. They were to be different from the other nations in that they would have only one God and only one temple. But the Israelites disobeyed the Lord and let the Canaanites remain in the land. They took up the worship of the many gods and goddesses of the nations and practiced their abominations. Their sins are cataloged in Psalm 106:36-40.

> They worshiped their idols, which became a snare to them. They sacrificed their sons and their daughters to demons. They shed innocent blood, the blood of their sons and daughters, whom they sacrificed to the idols of Canaan, and the land was desecrated by their blood. They defiled themselves by what they did; by their deeds they prostituted themselves. Therefore the LORD was angry with his people and abhorred his inheritance.

Besides the biblical accounts, we have no detailed *written* records of the religion of the Canaanites except for the myths and the ritual texts of their cousins far to the north at Ugarit. But we have abundant *archaeological* evidence of the idolatrous practices in the land of Canaan.

Places of Worship

The Canaanites had many temples to their gods and goddesses. Many of these have been excavated, for example, at Lachish,

Hazor, Megiddo, and Beth Shan. Some of these temples, notably a series at Beth Shan, also included Egyptian features for Egyptian soldiers garrisoned there, for Egyptian travelers, and perhaps also for Canaanites who chose to add Egyptian religious practices to their worship.

At Megiddo, over many centuries, a long series of Canaanite temples were built, one on top of the other. One of these, built near the end of the third millennium B.C., included a circular altar of fieldstones, more than 25 feet in diameter and 5 feet high. Seven steps led to the top of the altar, upon which sacrifices were offered. At the beginning of the second millennium B.C., a complex of three identical temples was added, forming an impressive Canaanite cultic precinct. Each of these temples consisted of a rectangular room with an altar platform at its back and an open courtyard at its entrance where a pair of round stone bases indicates pillars, perhaps similar to those of the Jerusalem temple. Toward the end of the second millennium B.C., a new Canaanite temple was built on the ruins of its predecessors. It had especially thick walls and included a small cultic chamber with two towers protecting its façade.

One of the most interesting temples in Canaan is the Philistine temple at Tel Qasile. The roof of this temple was supported by two closely placed pillars in the center of the sanctuary floor. It is an intriguing possibility to think that it was such central pillars that Samson destroyed to bring down the house. This presents quite a different picture than the common Sunday school illustrations in which it looks as if Samson is standing on the front steps of the First National Bank or the county courthouse.

Though there are some general architectural similarities between the temple in Jerusalem and Canaanite (Phoenician) temples, it was not the Canaanite temples that proved to be the great temptation for Israel. It was their small local shrines, "high places." These high places were not necessarily on a high hill or mountain, though many of them were. Another common location for high places was in or near the city gate. Many of these were open-air shrines.

Israelites worshiped alongside their Canaanite neighbors at shrines dedicated to the baals and the asherahs, or they built their own. However, many of the Israelite high places were not dedicated to Baal but to the Lord. These were illegitimate competitors of the Jerusalem temple. In our terms, these were heterodox high places rather than heathen ones.

The most notorious of these high places dedicated to the Lord were the shrines built at Bethel and Dan by the apostate King Jereboam for golden calf worship. He set these up to replace the Jerusalem temple. The base of the altar of his shrine at Dan has been discovered, and the high place there is partly restored.

Such illegitimate shrines, however, were not limited to the apostate north. They were also located in the royal administrative centers of Judah, such as Arad and Beersheba. The shrine at Arad is a miniature of the temple in Jerusalem, with a courtyard altar and a "holy of holies," small altars, and pillars. Such shrines were destroyed by the good kings Hezekiah and Josiah, but even the good kings could not rid the land of Judah of them.

One of the more intriguing finds is a stone platform on Mount Ebal, which the excavator identified as a ramped altar. Some have identified this either with the altar built at this site by Joshua or as a memorial to that event. But this is speculative, and many archaeologists question if it is even an altar.

Worship Paraphernalia and Practices

ALTARS

Pictures of the story of Cain and Abel often portray an altar bearing Abel's sacrifice, though the text does not specifically mention an altar. Noah built an altar, and Abraham, Isaac, and Jacob followed his example. Through Moses, God gave Israel specific directions for building such altars.

> Exodus 20:24-26. Make an altar of earth for me and sacrifice on it your burnt offerings and fellowship offerings, your sheep and goats and your cattle. Wherever I cause my name to be honored, I will come to you and bless you. If you make an altar of stones for me, do not build it with dressed stones, for you will defile it if you use a tool on it. And do not go up to my altar on steps, lest your nakedness be exposed on it.

The altars for the tabernacle and the temple did not follow this same pattern of using uncut stones. For these altars the Lord gave different specifications.

Exodus 27:1-8. Build an altar of acacia wood, three cubits high; it is to be square, five cubits long and five cubits wide. Make a horn at each of the four corners, so that the horns and the altar are of one piece, and overlay the altar with bronze. Make all its utensils of bronze—its pots to remove the ashes, and its shovels, sprinkling bowls, meat forks and firepans. Make a grating for it, a bronze network, and make a bronze ring at each of the four corners of the network. Put it under the ledge of the altar so that it is halfway up the altar. Make poles of acacia wood for the altar and overlay them with bronze. The poles are to be inserted into the rings so they will be on two sides of the altar when it is carried. Make the altar hollow, out of boards. It is to be made just as you were shown on the mountain.

The tabernacle altar was in a class by itself because it had to be portable. It was less than 5 feet high and 8 feet square. The temple altar was much bigger, about 15 feet high and 30 feet square (2 Chronicles 4:1). Josephus reports that the altar in Herod's temple was more than 20 feet high. Presumably the top was reached by a ramp.

None of these altars survive, though the base of the altar at Dan suggests an altar about half the size of the altar of Solomon's temple. The surviving stone altars are much smaller, similar in size to the tabernacle altar. Many surviving altars illustrate the "horns of the altar" that are mentioned frequently in the Old Testament. Blood from the sacrifices was placed on the horns of the altar (Leviticus 4:7,30), and those seeking asylum in the temple would cling to the horns of the altar (1 Kings 1:50,51).

The most interesting example of a surviving altar is an altar from Beersheba. This altar was not found intact but dismantled. Its well-dressed stones were found in secondary use in the walls of a later building. This has led to the suggestion that this altar may have been destroyed by King Hezekiah in his campaign to remove illegal places of worship from Judah (2 Kings 18:4). This altar has been reassembled, and the missing pieces have been restored. Several replicas are also on display in Israel. An interesting footnote to the discovery of this altar is that a former professor of Wisconsin Lutheran Seminary participated in its excavation.

King Josiah carried out a similar campaign to destroy illegal worship places.

> 2 Kings 23:12-15. He pulled down the altars the kings of Judah had erected on the roof near the upper room of Ahaz, and the altars Manasseh had built in the two courts of the temple of the LORD. He removed them from there, smashed them to pieces and threw the rubble into the Kidron Valley. The king also desecrated the high places that were east of Jerusalem on the south of the Hill of Corruption—the ones Solomon king of Israel had built for Ashtoreth the vile goddess of the Sidonians, for Chemosh the vile god of Moab, and for Molech the detestable god of the people of Ammon. Josiah smashed the sacred stones and cut down the Asherah poles and covered the sites with human bones. Even the altar at Bethel, the high place made by Jeroboam son of Nebat, who had caused Israel to sin—even that altar and high place he demolished. He burned the high place and ground it to powder, and burned the Asherah pole also.

In addition to the larger altars for sacrifice, many smaller habachi-sized altars, which probably served as incense altars, have been discovered. These too display the horns of the altar.

PILLARS

The Bible refers to the pillars or poles that often stood alongside the illegitimate altars. Some of these, especially those dedicated to the goddess Asherah, may have been wooden poles or tree trunks. Others were standing stones. These are called by the Hebrew name *matzeva* (plural *mazevot*). These apparently represented the deity. In Deuteronomy 16:21,22 the Lord prohibited such poles and sacred stones.

> Do not set up any wooden Asherah pole beside the altar you build to the LORD your God, and do not erect a sacred stone, for these the LORD your God hates.

The term *matzeva* ("erect stone") can also be used to refer to legitimate memorial stones, monuments, or grave markers (Genesis 28:18–22; 2 Samuel 18:18; Joshua 4:20–23; Genesis 35:20). But numerous *matzevot* have been discovered that seem to fit the category of forbidden *matzevot*. Most of these are plain stones with no writing or pictures on them.

Outside the city gate of Dan, five undressed stones about 2 feet tall were found standing erect. They apparently served as *matzevot*, marking a cultic place. The description of Josiah's reform again comes to mind: "He broke down the shrines at the gates" (2 Kings 23:8). Similar stones have been found next to the altar at the high place, or temple, of Arad.

Often tall, narrower stones are paired with shorter, wider stones. These are believed to represent the god and the goddess respectively. Often there are groups of stones (sometimes nine in number). These may represent pantheons of gods and goddesses.

A few standing stones, such as those found at Hazor, are finished stones. Most of these do not have writing or pictures on them, but one has praying hands reaching up toward the heavens.

Less clear in meaning is a row of seven or eight much taller (6 to 10 feet) standing stones from Gezer. Though some have associated these with a high place and attributed a phallic significance to them, others think they are more like the memorial stones that Israel erected to the 12 tribes (Exodus 24:4; Joshua 4:20). Perhaps they are not a unified set or monument but a gradual accumulation. They reinforce the point that the interpretation of such stones often involves a measure of speculation or conjecture.

VESSELS AND STANDS

A large number of clay pottery vessels, which were apparently used in worship, have been recovered from various shrines and temples. One of the most common forms is a stand with a bowl on the top, which looks somewhat like a birdbath. Some of these were incense burners. Others may have held liquids or plants.

Libations (the pouring out of liquids—water, milk, wine, beer, and perhaps blood) seem to have been an important part of

Canaanite worship, as they were in the worship of the temple. In connection with pagan sites, some very strange vessels have been found: bowls with hollow rims and hidden passages for the liquids, a hollow goddess with pierced breasts from which milk could stream. It is not known precisely how these were used. Some sites contain lined pits that apparently were receptacles for such libations.

An especially interesting find is a cache of vessels from En Hazeva in the Arabah, south of the Dead Sea on the way to Ezion Geber. This is believed to be a collection of Edomite vessels. The vessels were found smashed in a *favissa* (a buried deposit of cultic vessels). It appears that the vessels had been deliberately shattered by stones of various sizes, which were placed on top of the vessels after having been dismantled from a nearby shrine. The deposit consists of 63 complete pottery items and 7 stone altars of various sizes. There are 9 types of pottery items:

- 3 bizarre-looking anthropomorphic (human-shaped) stands that look more like extraterrestrials than people
- 8 stands, including one that served as the base for an anthropomorphic figure; some have incised designs, and some are decorated with figures
- 14 incense burners with fenestrated bases (bases with windows cut in them)
- 11 incense burners decorated with projecting triangles
- 11 small chalices
- 4 perforated cup-shaped incense burners
- 4 small bowls
- 2 incense shovels with projecting handles
- 2 types of pomegranate-shaped vessels (3 tiny, intact specimens and 3 larger ones)

This unique assemblage gives some hints of the strange goings-on that were part of Canaanite worship. It is attributed to the late seventh or early sixth century B.C. The smashing and burial of the vessels could be an honorable disposal and retirement, but some have associated it with a deliberate desecration, perhaps by a Judean king such as Josiah. At other sites, such as Hazor, idols were found beheaded, to put them out of commission.

Another interesting *favissa*, discovered in 2002 in a salvage excavation near Yavneh, is associated with a late stage of the Philistine culture. The vessels were apparently given an honorable burial after they were broken and no longer usable in the nearby temple. The deposit included regular pottery; unique rectangular cultic stands decorated with animal, human, and architectural elements; thousands of bowls and cubes; as well as other cult-related items. It included a fascinating mix of local Canaanite, Cypriote, Syrian, and other artistic elements—a witness to the eclectic nature of the Philistine culture and cult.

Human Sacrifice

There are many passages in the Old Testament condemning the human sacrifice practiced by the Canaanites and warning the Israelites against adopting this practice.

Some critics have tried to dismiss the frequent biblical references to "making the children pass through the fire" as some sort of consecration ceremony, like walking through lines of fire or walking on hot coals, but it is clear in Ezekiel 20:31 and Jeremiah 19:5 that the children were killed.

The king of Moab offered his firstborn son and heir as a whole burnt offering (*olah*) on the city wall in a desperate attempt to ward off Israel's attack (2 Kings 3:27). An Egyptian stone mural seems to picture a very similar scene that took place during an Egyptian siege of Ashkelon: On the top of the wall, the besieged inhabitants are raising their hands to heaven in supplication and burning incense. Two apparently lifeless children are being dangled from the wall. These two scenes give us insight into the sacrifice of children. It seems to have been a desperate measure, a last result when catastrophe was on the horizon.

The Bible says that the Ammonites offered child sacrifices to Moloch (also spelled Molech). His real name is probably a form of *Melek,* the word for "king," but the Israelites deliberately mispronounced it to mark it as shameful.

Tragically the Israelites adopted this shocking practice. The Israelites were forbidden to sacrifice any of their children to Moloch

(Leviticus 18:21 and 20:2-5), but Solomon built a high place for Moloch, the detestable god of the Ammonites, on the mountain across from Jerusalem (1 Kings 11:7). This was primarily for his heathen wives, but it introduced the vile cult into Israel. The wicked kings Ahaz and Manasseh were among those who sacrificed their sons in the fire (2 Kings 21:6 and 2 Chronicles 28:3). Josiah desecrated Topheth—the site of these sacrifices in the Valley of Ben Hinnom on the south side of Jerusalem—so no one could again use it to sacrifice his son or daughter in the fire of Moloch (2 Kings 23:10). But this action was too late. The practice of child sacrifice had made Topheth and Jerusalem into an abomination, and judgment was inevitable.

> They have built the high places of Topheth in the Valley of Ben Hinnom to burn their sons and daughters in the fire— something I did not command, nor did it enter my mind. So beware, the days are coming, declares the LORD, when people will no longer call it Topheth or the Valley of Ben Hinnom, but the Valley of Slaughter, for they will bury the dead in Topheth until there is no more room. (Jeremiah 7:31,32)

The term *tophet* (the usual spelling in archaeolgy), which became familiar as a place in Jerusalem, has become a technical term for sites of child sacrifice. The name is possibly derived from the Hebrew *toph*, "drum," because drums were used to drown the cries of the children, or more likely, from *taph* or *toph*, "to burn." Because of the abominations practiced there, *tophet* became a synonym for hell. *Gehenna* ("the Valley of Hinnom"), where the tophet was located, is one of Jesus' names for hell.

Commenting on Jeremiah 7:31, the 12th century rabbi Rashi explains Tophet:

> Tophet is Moloch, which was made of brass. They heated him from his lower parts, and when his hands were stretched out and made hot, they put the child between his hands, and it was burnt. When it vehemently cried out, the priests beat a drum, that the father might not hear the voice of his son, and his heart might not be moved.

Rashi seems here to confuse the location called Tophet with the idol Moloch, but his description of the idol as a giant fire pot is echoed in other sources. Another similar rabbinical tradition says that the idol was hollow and was divided into seven compartments, in one of which they put flour, in the second turtledoves, in the third a ewe, in the fourth a ram, in the fifth a calf, in the sixth an ox, and in the seventh a child. These then were all burned together by heating the statue from inside.

The Roman historian Diodorus Siculus reports a similar story concerning the Moloch of Carthage:

> In the temple there was an image of Chronos (Moloch), a human figure with a bull's head and outstretched arms. This image of metal was made glowing hot by a fire kindled within it, and the children laid in its arms rolled from there into the fiery lap below. If the children cried, the parents stopped their noise by fondling and kissing them, for the victim was not supposed to weep, and the sound of complaint was drowned in the din of flutes and drums. It is not certain whether the children were first slain or whether they were placed alive in the glowing arms of the image. *(Concerning Carthage)*

It is quite possible that the account of Diodorus is the point of origin of the story of the image, which was then picked up by Rashi and projected back into the land of Israel. This is not at all unreasonable since the Carthagians were Phoenicians who had migrated to North Africa. Phoenician was the Greek name for Canaanites. Thus there is a direct line of descent from the Canaanites to the Carthaginians.

At any rate, it is Carthage and other Phoenician cities in today's Lebanon that provide the main physical evidence for child sacrifice, evidence that, so far, is lacking in Israel. Carthage was notorious to its neighbors for child sacrifice. In additions to Diodorus, the historian Plutarch and the church father Tertullian mention the practice. Some critics try to dismiss the reports of Canaanite/Carthagian human sacrifice as propanda of their Israelite and Roman enemies, but archaeological evidence supports the charges.

Several apparent *tophets* have been identified, including a large one in Carthage. Excavations within Carthage and other Phoenician centers have revealed the burned remains of infants and children in large numbers. Most historians interpret this as evidence for frequent child sacrifice to the god Baal Hammon. Skeptics claim this was just a cemetery for cremated children. The archaeological evidence, however, especially the bones found inside the burial urns, cannot be so easily explained away: *stelae* ("stone pillars") associated with burial urns found at Carthage bear decorations alluding to sacrifice and inscriptions expressing vows to deities. These inscriptions, however, are highly formulaic and tantalizingly vague. None refers explicitly to child sacrifice, only to vows made to Tanit and Baal Hammon. For example, an inscription on a stele from the sixth to third century B.C. reads: "To our lady, to Tanit . . . and to our lord, to Baal Hammon, that which was vowed." The placement of such stelae immediately above the jars containing burned remains strongly suggests that these vows had something to do with the cremated individuals, human and/or animal, inside the jars. Moreover, the osteological (bone) evidence reveals that most of the victims were children two to three months old, though some were as old as age five. So far no skeleton has shown any signs of pathological conditions that might have caused death. These seem to have been healthy children deliberately killed as sacrifices in the manner described in the classical and biblical texts.

It is claimed that the worshipers placed their children alive in the arms of a bronze statue of the lady Tanit or the baal Moloch. The hands of these gods, it is said, extended over a brazier into which the children fell once the flames had caused the statues' limbs to move and its mouth to open. But all this is based on historical accounts, not on archaeological evidence. No such images have thus far been found. But the reluctance of the skeptics to believe the numerous reports of human sacrifice, a charge that the prophets of Israel make even against their own nation, seems to be evidence of some scholars' unwillingness to believe anything based even in part on the Bible.*

---

* For more information, see Lawrence E. Stager and Samuel R. Wolff, "Child Sacrifice at Carthage: Religious Rite or Population Control?" *Biblical Archaeology Review,* January/February 1984.

Gods and Goddesses

Baal was the most worshiped god of the Canaanites. Baal is not originally a proper name but a common noun meaning "lord," "master," or "owner." *Baalat* or *Baalah* is the feminine of baal and means "lady." Both terms are used to refer to deities.

Such gods as Melquart, Hadad, etc., were all varieties of baals. Hadad was the god's proper name; Baal was his title. There were many local baals—the Baal of Tyre, Baal Zaphon, Baal Zebub, etc.— just as there are many Mary's in Catholic worship, each named after a particular shrine—the Madonna of Guadalupe, etc.

Baal in his various manifestations seems to have been a storm and rain god and thus a god of fertility. The Ugartic myths contain the story of how Baal got a palace, that is, how he became a god worthy of his own temple.

Though Baal was the most worshiped god, he was not the head god. That would be his father, El. *El* is the Semitic word for "god."

The only other Canaanite god who plays a significant role in the Bible is Dagon, or Dagan, mentioned primarily as a god of the Philistines. Though sometimes associated with fish and the sea (the Hebrew word for "fish" is *dag*), Dagan seems to have been originally and primarily a grain god, worshiped especially in North Syria, including Ugarit, where he seems to be identified with El.

The identities of all these gods and of the goddesses who follow is rather fluid. At various times and places their roles seem to change and they tend to blend into one another.

The archaeological evidence for the gods is primarily twofold: the images of the seated god and of the smiting god.

The seated god sits on a throne. He often appears bareheaded and even bald. He often seems to be an older man. He is usually identified with El, but a crowned god, who looks more like Baal, sometimes occurs in the same seated posture.

The smiting god, usually identified with a manifestation of Baal, is standing with one arm upraised in a striking position. The weapon may now be missing from his hand, but it was usually some form of mace or club or even a lightning bolt. The god usually wears some form of crown, either a tall Egyptian-style crown or

71

some sort of horned helmet. These images are nearly always made of metal, most often bronze, and are sometimes plated with gold or silver.

Deities, including the smiting god, often stand on some sort of pedestal: a mountain or, most often, on the back of an animal. On one plaque of a baal, a god with lightning bolts in his hands stands on the back of a bull. This raises an intriguing possibility for understanding the golden calf. It was not so much intended to be a representation of the Lord but may have been the pedestal on which the invisible Lord was standing. A number of small, metal bull or calf images have been found in the land of Israel, but it is not certain if they were intended to be representations of gods or pedestals for gods. A very interesting and intriguing find is a cult stand from Tanaach that has several representations of gods and goddesses on it. In the middle, between a pair of cherubim, is a blank spot. Did a syncretizing Israelite leave this spot empty to represent the invisible Lord? Was the designer an idolater who worshiped other gods along with the Lord but still hesitated to represent the Lord with an image?

It does seem that the bull could represent the god. An unusual plaque from Geshur portrays a bull standing upright on two legs like a man or like an animal in a cartoon. This seems to represent a baal of some sort. He is much like the Moloch described above by Diodorus.

Other animals that serve as pedestals for deities (usually goddesses) are lions, cattle, and horses. One plaque of gold foil, for example, portrays a goddess standing on a horse's back like a circus' bareback rider.

Asherah was the main goddess worshiped in Israel. She was the mother goddess of the Canaanite pantheon. But just as there were many local baals, there were also many manifestations of Asherah. There is, in fact, a certain blurring and confusion of various goddesses as they are mixed and blended with one another.

Asherah seems to be the same as the Ugaritic Athirat, who is a mother goddess but is also associated with the sea at Ugarit, which was a maritime center. She is the wife/consort of El. At times she seems to be confused with Ashtart, who is the Mesopotamian Ishtar.

She is also called Elat, which is the feminine form of El, "god." The "Queen of Heaven," who is mentioned in the book of Jeremiah, seems to be identical with Asherah. In the Old Testament, this goddess has different manifestations since the plural, the Ashteroths, is used in reference to her.

When Ashtarte/Ashtart/Athtart is distinguished from Asherah, she has a more warlike and violent nature, though she too is associated with sexuality and fertility. Her symbols include the lion, the horse, the sphinx, the dove, and a star within a circle indicating the planet Venus. Pictorial representations often show her naked.

Anat, like Ashtarte, is a war goddess, but even more violent. In the Ugaritic myths, Anat appears as a wild and furious warrior in a battle—wading knee-deep in blood, striking off heads, cutting off hands, binding the heads to her body, and placing the hands in her sash as souvenirs—with her heart filled with joy. She is called a virgin but also is Baal's lover and sister. Anat does not appear as a goddess in the Old Testament, but her name occurs in place names in Israel and in the title of the judge Shamgar, so she was known in Israel (Judges 3:31).

In discussing the archaeological evidence for these goddesses, we will not attempt to distinguish them but will treat the Asherahs and Ashteroths as more or less interchangeable.

The most important evidence is the images of the goddess. These are found in all periods of history, from the earliest to the latest. The various styles of these images can in fact be used as a dating tool in the same way that pottery is. Most of the surviving images are not metal but clay, but this may be due to the recycling of metal images rather than to the original proportion of metal images to clay ones. The goddess is usually naked or near naked, and her form emphasizes her breasts, which she is often holding.

One rather grotesque clay image of the naked goddess from a very early period portrays her with a butter churn on her head, perhaps associating her with the fertility of the flocks.

An unusual metal image from the Bronze Age portrays the goddess with the gaunt figure of a super model. She wears a star-shaped crown. Actually, it was not the image itself that was found but the mold from which it could be mass produced.

The typical form during the Late Bronze Age (time of the judges) was the portrayal of the goddess on a flat plaque. Usually the goddess is naked except for a crown or headdress and an occasional belt. She holds plants (often lotuses) in her hands and often is standing on an animal or on the sun, moon, or stars. Sometimes goats are eating from the plants in her hands. Sometimes she is holding dead animals, apparently sacrifices, in her hands. A variant of this type of plaque is a gold necklace pendant that portrays the goddess in a stylized fashion. The plaque shows her head in relief, small breasts, a triangle that represents her sexual organs, and a tree branch. The triangle by itself can serve as her symbol.

A tree standing by itself can also serve as her symbol. A picture of two goats (a fertility animal) eating from the tree that stands between them is equivalent to the scene in which the goats are eating from the hands of the goddess. This tree, which represents the tree of life, is sometimes portrayed in a stylized manner, with seven branches like the Jewish menorah.

Two of the more unusual portrayals of the goddess from this period come from Philistine sites. One, already mentioned above, is a hollow vessel in the shape of the goddess who has pierced breasts from which liquid, presumably milk, could squirt. Similar vessels have been found at Phoenician sites. The breasts could be sealed with wax, and heated milk could be poured into the body of the goddess. The heat would melt the wax and a "miracle" would occur as the goddess spouted milk.

In the second unusual form, the goddess is portrayed as a high-backed chair that has breasts and a head. This form created an offering table of sorts onto which gifts to the goddess could be placed. In this portrayal, the head of the goddess is similar to those of Mycenaean (Greek) figurines of goddesses. This figure seems to be related to figurines from Cyprus in which the goddess is portrayed in full-bodied form but bent in a position like a person seated in a chair and with chair legs coming out of her posterior. In other words, the goddess could be portrayed as a chair with breasts and a head or as a woman with chair legs.

There are also clay figurines of pregnant women, whom some take as representations of the goddess, but these may represent women seeking her blessing of fertility.

Still another representation of the goddess were cakes made in her image. Jeremiah refers to such cakes.

Jeremiah 7:17,18. Do you not see what they are doing in the towns of Judah and in the streets of Jerusalem? The children gather wood, the fathers light the fire, and the women knead the dough and make cakes of bread for the Queen of Heaven. They pour out drink offerings to other gods to provoke me to anger.

Jeremiah 44:17-19. [The people say to Jeremiah,] "We will certainly do everything we said we would: We will burn incense to the Queen of Heaven and will pour out drink offerings to her just as we and our fathers, our kings and our officials did in the towns of Judah and in the streets of Jerusalem. At that time we had plenty of food and were well off and suffered no harm. But ever since we stopped burning incense to the Queen of Heaven and pouring out drink offerings to her, we have had nothing and have been perishing by sword and famine." The women added, "When we burned incense to the Queen of Heaven and poured out drink offerings to her, did not our husbands know that we were making cakes like her image and pouring out drink offerings to her?"

Archaeological evidence for this practice is a "cake pan" in the shape of the goddess, but with openings where her nose, breasts, and sex organs should be—apparently to allow for a 3-D effect at these parts of her image.

The Iron Age (period of the kings) form of her image is different. It is not a plaque but a free-standing image. The head, formed in a mould, has a hairstyle that may reflect the style of upper class ladies of the day. The breasts are full-figured, but the lower part of her body from the breasts down is a cylinder that resembles a tree trunk. This may be another indication of a connection between the goddess and a tree. The importance of this type of image is that it is found in the destruction layer of Jerusalem and shows one reason why the city was destroyed.

In a variant of the goddesss-as-tree theme, worshipers are portrayed as being nursed by a tree with breasts. Also, at times worshipers are nursed by a cow, which represents the goddess.

A late manifestation of the mother goddess is Diana of the Ephesians. She is not the Diana of the classical myths but an Eastern mother goddess. She is called Polymastos, the many-breasted. Her images, which are found also in the land of Israel, seem to be many-breasted, though some have argued that the many ovals that cover her chest are ostrich eggs, bull testicles, or some other symbol of fertility.

Understanding the nature of this goddess and her worship helps make it clear why the Lord did not want his people to tolerate the Canaanites but to drive them out of their land.

Yahweh's Asherah

A couple of cryptic texts seem to refer to Yahweh's Asherah. (*Yahweh* is the presumed pronunciation of the Hebrew name for the Lord.) An eighth century B.C. ostracon discovered by Israeli archeologists at Quntilat Ajrud during excavations in the Sinai desert in 1975, prior to the Israeli withdrawal, is translated: "I have blessed you by YHVH of Samaria and his Asherah." Another inscription, from Khirbet el-Kom near Hebron, has been translated: "Blessed be Uriyahu by Yahweh and by his Asherah; from his enemies he saved him!" Some scholars have suggested that Asherah in these texts is Yahweh's wife. Is this possible? It is certainly possible that the Israelites who were mixing polytheism with the true faith would give the Lord a wife so he would be just like the other gods. We have already noted the cult stand from Tanaach that seems to allow a place for the Lord among the other gods and goddesses. Nevertheless, this interpretation of the text is not very well grounded.

For one thing, the translation of the text is far from certain. But even if we would grant the translation "Yahweh and his Asherah," it would not follow that this was understood as Yahweh's wife. The word *asherah* also refers to a sacred tree or pole that stood near shrines to honor Asherah. When the word refers to an object rather than a goddess, the Hebrew plural is a masculine form rather than a feminine. In Judges, Gideon ordered an Asherah pole next to an altar to Baal to be cut down and the wood to be used for a burnt offering.

In other situations, *asherah* may refer to a living tree or a grove of trees or the shrine inside such a grove. Many older translations render *asherah* as "grove." Since syncretizing Israelites worshiped the Lord not only in the legitimate temple but in local shrines like Baal's, it is possible, perhaps even likely, that Yahweh's local shrines either had an asherah or perhaps even were an asherah.

The Bible frequently denounces both Asherah and asherahs. Deuteronomy 16:21,22 reads: "Do not set up any wooden Asherah pole beside the altar you build to the LORD your God, and do not erect a sacred stone, for these the LORD your God hates." Bad kings of Israel set up asherahs. Good kings destroyed them. King Manasseh, for example, is said to have placed an Asherah pole in the temple, and he, therefore, was one who "did much evil in the eyes of the LORD" (2 Kings 21:6), but good king Hezekiah "removed the high places, smashed the sacred stones and cut down the Asherah poles" (2 Kings 18:4). He was, therefore, the most righteous of Judah's kings before the coming of the reformer Josiah, who also destroyed many Asherah poles (2 Kings chapter 23). If Yahweh had an asherah, it seems it was more likely a shrine than a wife.

Speaking of shrines, archaeology has uncovered other evidence of local idolatry in the form of little clay houses for the gods and goddesses, similar to our manger sets.

The presence of masks in some temples suggests that priests did some role-playing. Other masks, however, seem the right size for images.

The archaeological evidence supports the biblical statements about Israel's apostasy and idolatry, but this is a description of what they did, not of what they were supposed to do. Israelite polytheism was not a lower stage from which monotheism evolved, but it was a decline and backsliding from what they had been given by the one true Lord.

BURIAL

One of the traits that sets human beings apart from animals is our spiritual nature, which leads to a reverent treatment of the dead based on the belief that human life continues even after the death of the body. Among the heathen, this belief went in two directions: reverent honor of the dead because the living sought their favor (today, the veneration of the saints) and fear of the spirits of the dead, which led to magic and spells to protect against them (today, the occult).

The three big issues of human life on earth are food, sex, and death. These are the three issues that God addressed with Adam and Eve in the garden (in the sweat of your brow you will earn food; in pain you will bear children; you will return to the ground you came from). These three big aspects of life are points of emphasis in natural religions. In the previous chapter, we saw how the Israelites slid into a polytheistic way of dealing with sex and fertility. Did they also pick up on the heathen way of dealing with death? We have biblical evidence that some of them turned to occult methods of communicating with the spirits of the dead—for example, Saul. The Israelites seem also to have partaken in heathen feasts for the dead. But we have no direct archaeological evidence for these practices, so here we will focus our attention, for the most part, on their burial practices.

Differences in burial practice may reflect ethnic or religious traditions (for example, the general aversion of Christians to cremation until relatively recently), economic and social status (the pyramids of the pharaohs versus simple pit graves of the poor), or different time periods. For the most part, our study of burial practices in biblical times will be chronological.

Pre-Israel

We have archaeological evidence for the burial practices of pre-Israelite peoples in Palestine. Early burials in the Golan Heights area of the northern Transjordan are marked with large stone markers called dolmens. These resemble a miniature Stonehenge. Two upright vertical stones a couple of feet high are topped by a large, thick horizontal stone that lies across them like the top of a table.

Other burials were in small house-like mausoleums called charnal houses. This form is found at sites near the Dead Sea, which some have associated with Sodom and Gomorrah.

Other people buried their dead under the floors of their houses. A strange custom during the very early phases of Jericho and other places far to the north was the preservation of the skulls of ancestors, which were covered with plaster and given eyes made of shells.

Some of Israel's predecessors and neighbors practiced cremation. The remains were often deposited in large jars.

Since none of these forms had a direct influence on Israel, we will note them only in passing as evidence for the near universal practice of special treatment for the dead.

Israelite Burial Practices

At various times the Israelites buried their dead in simple graves in the earth, in caves, and in constructed tombs. In the early periods, we cannot necessarily distinguish Israelite burials from those of their neighbors, so we will make no effort to make a sharp distinction between them.

During most periods in Israel, most people, except for the most well-to-do, were buried in simple graves dug in the ground. Sometimes these graves were lined or covered with stone. Burial was usually with the body wrapped but with no coffin. Grave goods—such as pottery, jewelry, or weapons—sometimes accompanied the burials.

Other peoples did use coffins. A Late Bronze Age cemetery near Gaza yielded many clay coffins in an Egyptian style. They are called anthropoid coffins because, as on the coffins of the pharaohs, the face of the deceased is modeled on the cover, but in a much cruder fashion. The best of these coffins were probably for Egyptians living in Canaan, but some at other sites could be for Canaanites emulating

Egyptian fashion. The coffins were placed in graves cut into the sandstone or red clay. Almost all were oriented west to the sunset. Discovered in these coffins were large quantities of alabaster vessels; Ushabti figurines (little models buried with Egyptians); scarabs; gold jewelry; beads of precious stones and gold; and pottery of Mycenaean, Cypriot, Egyptian, and local Canaanite types. Some coffins contained more than one burial, perhaps husband and wife.

Another form of coffin is called the bathtub coffin because it looks like a clay bathtub. This form seems to be an adaptation of a Mesopotamian form.

Except in the driest climates, wood coffins would have rotted and disappeared. Evidence for their existence would be nails appropriately spaced around the body.

A variant of these simple pit graves are shaft graves. At the bottom of a rather deep shaft, a small chamber is cut off to the side. It is sealed with stone.

In a more elaborate form of shaft tomb, there is a vertical shaft, but at the bottom, cut into the rock, are several burial chambers extending in different directions. Each of these are sealed by stones and can be entered individually at different times without disturbing other recent burials. These tombs are in a sense small artificial caves. This form was common in the Middle Bronze period.

The Israelites also placed their dead in caves. We have reference to this practice already among the patriarchs, who buried their dead in the Cave of Machpelah (Genesis 23:17-20). These caves were often family tombs used by many family members over a long period of time. Israelites were "gathered to their fathers" not only spiritually but physically. Grave goods such as pottery vessels of various sorts, jewelry, and weapons were placed with the dead. This makes such tombs of interest both to archaeologists and tomb robbers. A practice that seems strange to us is that those who used these tombs did not seem to have much compunction about moving the bones of ancestors to a pile in the corner to make room for new arrivals.

Natural caves could be enhanced by enlarging or shaping the chamber by excavating the soft limestone. Artificial caves could be created by cutting tombs into the rock. Some of these are quite elaborate. An entry is cut into a face of the cliff or the quarry wall. Then one or more rectangular burial rooms is cut into the rock. One of the most interesting examples is found near the Garden Tomb, just north of the northern wall of the Old City of Jerusalem on the grounds of Ecole Biblique—the French biblical and archaeological society in Jerusalem. A central court is surrounded by eight burial chambers. The

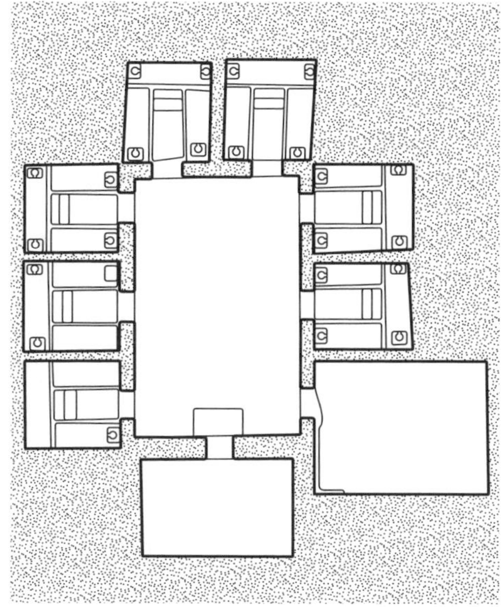

Elaborate cave tomb

usual form of a burial chamber is a "bed" cut into the rock along each of the non-entry walls of the room. Beds sometimes have horseshoe-shaped pillows cut into the stone. Under the bed is a chamber cut into the rock into which the bones of the deceased can be placed after the flesh is gone. This tomb could accommodate 24 in the beds and hundreds in the bone chambers. This tomb, constructed during the period of the Israelite monarchy, was reused as late as the Byzantine period.

Other less elaborate tombs of this type are found all around Jerusalem, notably on the east side of the Kidron Valley, across from the City of David. These are most likely the tombs of the nobility of the Old Testament period. One of these tombs has an inscription that may link it with the royal steward Shebna, whose tomb is mentioned in Isaiah chapter 22. A tomb at the southwest corner of the city yielded a small silver scroll, which contained a version of the Aaronic Benediction, to be worn as a necklace. The lower level of some rock-cut tombs, which may be the tombs of the kings, have been found on the west side of the Kidron Valley. But unfortunately, in later times quarrying destroyed most of the upper portions of these tombs.

Jesus' Tomb

Jesus' tomb was a later variety of the artificial cave tomb discussed previously. The Garden Tomb just north of the Old City is almost surely not the tomb of Christ but merely a simpler version of the Old Testament tomb on the grounds of the Ecole Biblique. The Garden Tomb is, in fact, part of the same cemetery. It has only one of the three-bed side chambers with the stone pillows. Though it was probably reused in the New Testament time period or later, it could not be Christ's tomb because his was a new tomb that had never been used before (Luke 23:53).

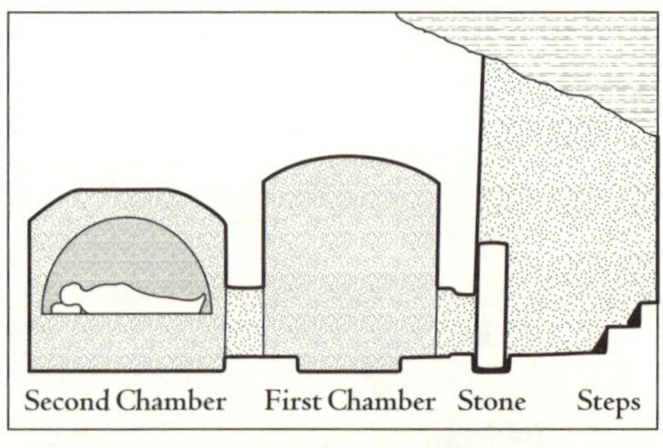

Tomb Sealed With a Stone

The Garden Tomb preserves some of the atmosphere of Christ's tomb, a rock-cut tomb near the city, but the tomb's construction is much too early. The rolling stone that once was present is gone from the channel. For the real location and a better view of the tomb, we will have to look elsewhere.

It is likely that the real location of Christ's tomb is at the Church of the Holy Sepulchre. Though this church is now within the walls of the Old City, the archaeological evidence of tombs under the church supports the idea that it was outside the city at the time of Jesus. The tomb would have been cut into the rock face of what was probably a cliff created by quarrying.

When Constantine built a church and courtyard around the tomb in A.D. 326, he probably had his crews cut away much of the cliff in which the tomb was cut, leaving only a standing cube of rock. The rectangular structure that stands under the great dome today approximates that original tomb. The tomb itself was reportedly destroyed by a Muslim ruler in about A.D. 1000. Remnants of its walls may remain inside the present structure, which is called the Aedicule. This little building may need to be disassembled soon because of its state of disrepair. It will be interesting to see if traces of the tomb remain. Further east, near the present entrance of the church, there is a standing rock that is identified with Golgotha.

It seems that this site is likely to be authentic (though the site of Golgotha may have lain somewhat to the south of the church) for the following reasons:

- The site was outside the city at Jesus' time, as would be necessary.
- The site was in the city at the time when the church was built, making it unlikely that the identification was just made up to satisfy Constantine. In that case, a site outside Jerusalem would most likely have been chosen.
- Pre-Constantine pilgrim journals support this as being the true site.
- To build his church, Constantine had to tear down a Roman temple that had been built on the site in the second century—a drastic measure if there had not been a great deal of certainty about the site.
- There seems to have been continuous Christian memory of the site.

So for our best chance to visit the site of Christ's tomb, we should visit the Church of the Holy Sepulchre. But for the best view of what the tomb was like, we might visit other local tombs. There are several tombs in the Jerusalem area that still have a rolling stone like that of Jesus' tomb. These stones are not big boulders but carefully cut circular disks, similar in shape to a jar lid. Some stones simply roll in a stone channel in front of the tomb wall. Some are dropped into a slot cut into the cliff. Some have an artificial wall constructed in front of the stone.

My favorite example of this kind of tomb—that is easily accessible—is a tomb probably constructed for Herod's family. It is located in Liberty Bell Park near the King David Hotel west of the Old City. To enter this tomb, one descends a few steps. The circular stone is set into a slot cut into the rock. Several large rectangular rooms make up the tomb. Formerly these chambers were open to visitors with their own flashlights, but the last time I was there, a metal door blocked entry.

During the Intertestamental Period and later, some tombs were cut entirely free of the rock so that they stood like little buildings within the cliff. Sometimes steeple-like structures were added to the tops of the tombs that extended above the upper surface of the cliff. Three outstanding examples of such tombs are found near the southeast corner of the Old City.

Another feature of Jewish burial of the time period were ossuaries, or bone boxes. These small limestone boxes were just big enough to contain the longest bone in the human body. After the flesh had decomposed, the bones were gathered and placed into the box, freeing a portion of the tomb for reuse. One of these ossuaries is inscribed with the name of Caiphas and another with the name of James, the brother of Jesus. This controversial find will be discussed in the chapter on frauds and forgeries.

One controversial aspect of the excavation of tombs is the treatment of the bones found in them. The bones are valuable for archaeologists. They can yield information about the age of the deceased at death, their sex, perhaps ethnic affinities (though this is problematic), and some information about their health and diet. As is the case with Native American burials in North America, this is a very controversial topic because some people want either no excavation of burials at all or immediate reburial of the bones. This has led to some conflict between archaeologists and Orthodox Jews who oppose excavation of Jewish burials and any retention of bones for study. Most groups have fewer scruples about the study of bones of peoples other than their own, but even the display of Egyptian mummies has become a subject of some controversy.

They say that Money talks. This is certainly true in archaeology. Archaeologists can learn a lot from coins. Coins found in a secure locus can help date the locus. Coins can help trace trade patterns. Whether or not coins have been debased by diluting the percentage of precious metal they contain is a measure of economic health. The pictures and mottos on coins were an important method of propaganda in ancient societies such as Persia, Greece, and Rome.

Coins did not come into use until near the very end of the Old Testament. The monetary references in the Old Testament are to weights of precious metal and not to coins. Shekel, minas, and talents are measures of weight. Archaeologists have found examples of the weight sets that were used to measure out payment. Sometimes these sets are simple, undecorated, dome-shaped weights of various sizes, but occasionally they are more decorative. For example, a set of lion-shaped weights of various sizes has been found.

There were probably some standard-size ingots, but payment was sometimes made simply by weighing out quantities of cut-up precious metal, known by its German name *Hacksilber*. Gold and silver jewelry was also a form of portable wealth. A woman's jewelry could serve as divorce insurance and as life insurance on her husband.

A perpetual problem, of course, was dishonest weights. This form of thievery is mentioned several times in the Old Testament. A solution was to mark weights of metal with a guaranteed weight. This is what a precious metal coin is. It's a little ingot with a guarantee stamp on it.

Standard coinage seems to have begun in the kingdom of Lydia, in present-day Turkey, under the legendary King Croesus. The Persian Empire was the first empire with a widely circulated series of gold and silver coins. Alexander the Great and his successors issued beautiful coins featuring their portraits and symbols of their accomplishments, for example, war elephants. The coins of respected economic powers circulated widely. The Athenian silver coins, called owls because of the picture of Athena's owl on them, were widely circulated along the whole eastern shore of the Mediterranean.

The first Judean coins were knock-offs of popular Persian or Greek designs that were over-stamped with the word *Yehud*, "Judea."

The Hasmonean kings, relatively independent rulers of Israel under Roman protection just before the New Testament era, issued their own small bronze coins, but not silver or gold coins. For these, foreign issues were still the standard. Because of Jewish sensibilities against idolatry, Jewish coins could not feature the portrait of the ruler. The coins had simple pictures of plants, anchors, and horns of plenty. The reverse sides featured an inscription of the king, which emphasized his title of high priest. These inscriptions used the archaic form of the Hebrew alphabet, which was no longer in common use. Some of their later issues included religious objects, like the menorah and temple vessels. Some of their coins used the title "king," but in Greek rather than Hebrew.

Small Bronze Coins

The Herods and the Roman governors who followed the Hasmonians continued the practice of issuing only small bronze coins without portraits. The coins of the Herods retained many of the same motifs as the Hasmonean coins but without the Hebrew inscriptions. For the most part, the Roman governors stuck to unoffensive motifs like grain and grape leaves, which would not offend the Jews. The notable exception was Pilate. True to his reputation for crudity and lack of tact, he put heathen symbols, such as a magician's wand, on the coins he issued in Jerusalem. These coins are quite popular with collectors since they are dated, and some of them are dated to A.D. 30, the likely year of Christ's death. The date on these coins is an abbreviation that looks like the letters *LIZ*.

All of these very small bronze coins were commonly called mites in older English translations. The more technically correct name would be *lepton* (Greek) or the somewhat larger *prutah* (Hebrew).

The widow's mites could be any of these small coins, much smaller than a penny.

For gold and silver coins, the Jews continued to depend on the mints of their gentile neighbors. Two of these silver coins played a significant role in biblical history.

The first is the Roman silver denarius. This is the coin Jesus used when responding to the Jews challenge, "Is it right to pay taxes to Caesar or not?" (Matthew 22:17,19 and Mark 12:15). Jesus asked to see one of the coins that the Jews were happy to use. On one side of the coin was the portrait of the emperor Tiberius and his imperial title "Augustus Tiberius, son of the Divine Augustus." Jesus' answer, "Give to Caesar what is Caesar's" (Mark 12:17), means that if the Jews were happy to use Tiberius' coins and economic system, they should pay the taxes that supported that system.

The more interesting part of the story may lie on the back of the coin. The picture there is of Livia, the scheming mother of Tiberius, but it may be an image of the goddess of peace. There is also the inscription "Pontifex Maximus," translated "high priest." On the front of his coin, Tiberius was claiming to be the ruler of the state, and on the back, the head of its religion. Jesus' answer, "Give to Caesar what is Caesar's and to God what is God's," granted Caesar the honor he claimed on the one side but denied him the honor he claimed on the other.

The second important silver coin is the shekel of the Phoenician city of Tyre. This highly regarded shekel and its corresponding half shekel were the coins required for the temple tax by the temple authorities (the temple tax was a half shekel per man). Older commentaries sometimes say that worshipers had to go to the temple money changers in order to change their gentile money with its offensive images for clean Jewish coinage. One reason that this would have been impossible is that there was no Jewish silver and gold coinage at this time. But the reality is even worse. The temple authorities were actually demanding Baal money as the standard of the temple. They placed economic gain well above religious sensibility: The portrait featured on the coin was Melquart, the Tyrian version of Baal, and the reverse design was the Tyrian eagle and the city motto "Tyre holy and inviolable." (Some of the later issues of these coins may be knockoffs minted in Jerusalem because the Romans were debasing the currency of Tyre.)

This coin may appear as many as three times in the gospel narratives. Since it was the standard currency of the temple, it was the chief currency of the money changers Jesus drove out of the temple (Matthew 21:12). Since it was the chief temple currency, these were likely the coins with which the treachery of Judas was rewarded and with which the Field of Blood was purchased (the text refers only to "thirty silver coins" [Matthew 26:15]). The coin that Peter extracted from the fish to pay the temple tax for himself and Jesus was also quite possibly a shekel of Tyre (Matthew 17:27).

The Jews first issued their own silver coins during their two revolts from Rome in A.D. 66–70 and A.D. 132. These coins are an excellent demonstration of the propaganda value of coins. Whereas the shekels of Tyre bore the motto of Tyre, these coins carried the motto "Jerusalem the Holy." The other motto, "Shekel of Israel," declared that the Jews were now minting their own shekels for the temple tax. Mottos on other coins of the revolt included "Freedom of Zion" and "For the Redemption of Zion." The mottos were in archaic Hebrew. The dates on the coins help monitor the progress of the revolt. There were no portraits but rather items like pomegranates and temple vessels.

Sadly, Rome won both the military war and the propaganda war. After the destruction of Jerusalem, the Romans issued a massive minting of gold, silver, and bronze coins with the motto "Judea Capta," "Judah Captured." The picture was of a forlorn woman sitting under a palm tree, representing Judah in Roman captivity. The other side featured the portrait of the victorious emperors Titus and Vespasian.

In A.D. 132, in an attempt to regain Jerusalem and rebuild the city and temple, the Jews revolted again. Once again coins were instruments of propaganda. Among the motifs are the temple with the ark with a star rising over it, musical instruments of the temple, and vessels of the temple. Mottos include "The Year of Redemption" and the names of some of the leaders of the revolt. The most notorious leader of the revolt was Simon Bar Kochba, one of the false messiahs whom Christ warned against. *Bar Kochba* means "Son of the Star" (an allusion to the messianic prophecy of Balaam in Numbers chapter 24). The star above the temple may point to Bar Kochba. Not all the coins have the star, so one of the intriguing questions is whether the coins without the star predate his rising or are they an omen that his star had set?

A second propaganda coup of these coins was due to the fact that they were not struck on blanks but were over-strikes of Roman coins. The result was that traces of the emperor's face could sometimes still be seen crushed under the Jewish design. This may simply have been the result of the limitations of minting with a hand-hammered die, but I would like to think it was an "in your face" gesture.

But again the Romans had the last laugh both militarily and numismatically. The revolt was crushed, and the name Jerusalem was wiped off the map. Coins were issued with the new name of the city: *Aelia Capitolinea* in honor of the emperor's family. This was the end of Jewish coinage from Jerusalem until the modern restoration of Israel. For centuries the coins of Jerusalem alternated. First they were Christian and then Islamic, then Christian again during the crusades, then again Islamic, and finally British.

There is little physical archaeological evidence that can be connected directly to Jesus, though the traditional identification of many of the sites of his life may well be correct. A number of items associated with his life have already been discussed in the preceding chapters. For the most part, in such cases I will simply refer to that discussion and provide a brief recap.

Bethlehem

What about the archaeology of Christmas? Earlier chapters referred to the tradition that the stable was a cave. The Christian apologist Justin Martyr (who died about A.D. 165) reported this tradition in his *Dialogue With Trypho:*

> Joseph took up his quarters in a certain cave near the village; and while they were there, Mary brought forth the Christ and placed him in a manger, and here the Magi who came from Arabia found him. (chapter LXXVIII)

A certain amount of skepticism about the precision of his information is justified by the fact that it is unlikely that the Magi came from Arabia or that they visited Jesus on Christmas in the stable (our manger sets notwithstanding). The cave tradition is repeated by other church fathers. Origen of Alexandria (who died about 254) wrote:

> There is shown at Bethlehem the cave where he was born, and the manger in the cave where he was wrapped in swaddling-clothes. And this sight is greatly talked of in surrounding places, even among the enemies of the faith, it being said that in this cave was born that Jesus who is worshipped and reverenced by the Christians. (*Contra Celsum,* book I, chapter 51)

It is possible to visit stable-caves near Bethlehem that are very similar to the stable in which the Lord was born. There are also clay mangers and stone mangers that are undoubtedly very similar to the manger in which Christ was laid. But at the supposed site of his birth in Bethlehem, the archaeological evidence has been obscured by the building of the Church of the Nativity.

The Church of the Nativity, however, is interesting in its own right. It is one of the oldest churches in Christendom. The first basilica on this site, begun by Helena, the mother of the Emperor Constantine, was completed in A.D. 333. That church was burned down in the Samaritan Revolt of 529. The current church was rebuilt in 565 by the Emperor Justinian I. When the Persians invaded Palestine in 614 and destroyed many of the churches, they unexpectedly spared the Church of the Nativity. According to legend, their commander was moved by the depiction inside the church of the magi wearing Persian clothing and commanded that the building be spared.

The present-day church is actually two churches side by side: the main Basilica of the Nativity, under the jurisdiction of the Greek Orthodox, and the adjoining Church of St. Catherine, a Roman Catholic church. Of interest to us is the Grotto of the Nativity, which lies below the basilica. It is the alleged remnant of the cave where Jesus is said to have been born. The "exact spot" is marked beneath an altar by a 14-pointed silver star set into the marble floor and surrounded by silver lamps. This altar is denominationally neutral, although it is primarily Armenian in style. Another altar in the Grotto, which is maintained by the Roman Catholics, marks the site where, according to tradition, Mary laid the newborn baby in the manger. Of the fifteen lamps burning around the site, six belong to the Greeks, five to the Armenians, and four to the Latins. Any archaeological authenticity of the site is obscured by the competing sects who contend over it. Even less edifying is the nearby Milk Grotto, where Mary allegedly spilled some milk while nursing Jesus when she was hiding from Herod's soldiers. The milk turned the rocks of the cave a chalk-white color. The rock is believed to have healing power and to make it easier for women to nurse.

Nazareth

Nazareth today is an Arab city nestled in a natural bowl in the hills of Galilee. About one-third of the population is Christian, but like Christians throughout Israel and Palestine, they are under Muslim pressure. The Israeli part of the town is on the hills above.

The present-day Church of the Annunciation is an impressive Roman Catholic structure built in the 1960s over the remains of older churches. On the lower level of the church are remains from an ancient church and the grotto (cave) where Gabriel appeared to Mary. (Does anyone notice a pattern here?) Shut out from this church, the Orthodox identify a nearby spring, the Well of Mary, as the place of Gabriel's appearance. A nearby church is associated with the home of Joseph. Sorry, not much archaeological help here.

Capernaum

Fortunately, things begin to look up archaeologically when we arrive in Capernaum, on the north shore of the Sea of Galilee. Capernaum was Jesus' third home—Bethlehem was his birth town, Nazareth was his boyhood home, and Capernaum was his home during his ministry.

One reason Jesus left Nazareth was because of the unbelief of most of the inhabitants. But after a brief period of popularity, he encountered much hostility and rejection also in the towns by the lake. Perhaps a more significant reason for relocating to Capernaum was its strategic location as a center for preaching the gospel. It was on a crossroads. The surrounding countryside and lakeshore were well-populated. Whereas some have estimated the population of Nazareth to be as low as five hundred people and so insignificant that it is barely mentioned in Jewish sources, Capernaum and the area around the lake had a population of many thousands.

The most impressive archaeological find in Capernaum is its synagogue. It is constructed of white stone rather than the black basalt typical of construction in the area, and it has been impressively restored. The synagogue of Capernaum figured prominently in the ministry of Jesus. This restored building, however, is from the fourth or fifth century A.D. Underneath the restored synagoge there is evidence of an earlier synagogue that could be the synagogue mentioned in the gospels (Mark 1:21-28; Mark 5:22; Luke 4:33; Luke 7:1-5; Luke 8:41; John 6:25-59).

The second major attraction is the "house of Peter." The foundations of a 5th century octagonal church are built over the remains of a courtyard house of the 1st century, which tradition identifies as the house of Peter. The site may have been converted to a house-church before the construction of the octagonal church. Whether this house was or was not the house of Peter, it seems clear that the people who built the church over it believed that it was. The ambiance of the area is spoiled by a flying-saucer-shaped church, which the Franciscans, who maintain the site, have suspended over the ruins.

A number of interesting finds are scattered around the grounds, including the large millstone mentioned earlier.

Another attraction at Capernaum is sailing on the sea in a reconstruction of the so-called Jesus Boat. There will be more about this later in chapter 10 on underwater archaeology. Evidence of the fishing industry is also apparent in the facilities and small harbors around the lake.

Other Towns of the Lake

BETHSAIDA

Three apostles—Peter, Andrew, and Philip—were from Bethsaida, and many events of Jesus' ministry occurred in the vicinity of this town.

In recent years there have been significant excavations at what I will call the new Bethsaida. This site, known as et-Tell, is more than a mile from the present shore of the sea, but some studies have stated that in the past it was on the lakeshore. Some still vigorously dispute the identification of Bethsaida with et-Tell and argue for a site nearer the present lakeshore. The Iron Age city, which underlies the New Testament era city, is probably the Geshur of the Old Testament.

The most significant find for our purposes is the so-called House of the Fisherman, so named because two types of lead net weights, a long crooked needle, fish hooks, and anchors were discovered there.

KORAZIN

Korazin (Chorazin) was situated north of Capernaum, about 2 miles from the sea. It has a dramatic view of the sea, 900 feet below. The ruins of the city are mostly constructed from the black volcanic basalt typical of the area. The synagogue has been partially reconstructed. Though there is some dispute about the date, it appears to have been built after Christ. Among the carvings and stone works recovered from the ruins is a stone chair, apparently for synagogue dignitaries, which has been named "Moses' Seat" in reference to Jesus' remark.

Matthew 23:2,3. The teachers of the law and the Pharisees sit in Moses' seat. So you must obey them and do everything they tell you. But do not do what they do, for they do not practice what they preach.

Other interesting finds on the site include olive presses, which might be an indication of a major industry of the site. The city is best known for its association with Capernaum and Bethsaida in Jesus' solemn warning.

Matthew 11:21-24. Woe to you, Korazin! Woe to you, Bethsaida! If the miracles that were performed in you had been performed in Tyre and Sidon, they would have repented long ago in sackcloth and ashes. But I tell you, it will be more bearable for Tyre and Sidon on the day of judgment than for you. And you, Capernaum, will you be lifted up to the skies? No, you will go down to the depths. If the miracles that were performed in you had been performed in Sodom, it would have remained to this day. But I tell you that it will be more bearable for Sodom on the day of judgment than for you.

All of these cities were destroyed and remained uninhabited ruins for centuries. The ruins lie as a sad testimony to Jesus' words.

Other sites around the sea associated with Jesus' ministry are marked by churches old and new, but there is little of direct archaeological significance at those sites. They do provide information about where early pilgrims thought the sites of events in Jesus' ministry were located, but not much else. The murals or mosaics often portray the event that was believed to have happened at each site. Most of the site identifications are plausible. A few are not.

Jerusalem

Some of the preceding topical chapters have already discussed important archaeological findings that cast light on Jesus' ministry in Jerusalem. Here we will just cross-reference them.

- The Pool of Bethesda and the Pool of Siloam are discussed in chapter 4 on water systems.
- The coins that appear in the gospels (the widow's mite, the tribute to Caesar, the pieces of silver, and Pilate's coins) are discussed in chapter 7 on coins.
- Jesus' tomb is discussed in chapter 6 on burials.

THE TEMPLE MOUNT

Jews divide their biblical history into two periods: the First Temple Period and the Second Temple Period. The First Temple Period is the Old Testament period from the time of Solomon in the 900s B.C. to the destruction of the first temple in 586 B.C. by the Babylonians. The second temple—built by the Jews who returned from Babylon with Joshua the high priest and Zerubbabel the prince of Judah—was completed in about 520–516 B.C. This temple stood until A.D. 70 when it was destroyed by the Romans. Herod's temple, which was the temple Jesus visited, was such a complete rebuilding of the second temple that for all practical purposes it could have been called the third temple.

Herod the Great began a massive expansion of the Temple Mount and construction of a completely new and much larger temple complex around 19 B.C. Work on this project continued for many years. Although the structure of the second temple was completely removed and a new third temple was built to replace it, Herod's temple is not called the third temple because the sacrifices were never interrupted throughout the construction process and because the Jews were not eager to give credit to Herod, whom they hated.

This temple was the greatest of Herod's many magnificent building projects, but nothing of the temple itself still stands. As Jesus said, "Not one stone here will be left on another" (Matthew 24:2). Now nothing remains intact except the huge platform that Herod built to enlarge the area for the temple complex.

It is important that we distinguish between the temple and the temple complex. As a layman Jesus could not enter the temple proper, which was entered only by the ministering priests. The temple itself was a rather small building in proportion to the vast area of the open courts, porches, and colonnades that surrounded it. All of Jesus' visits to "the temple" were only to the outer parts of the temple complex, to the courtyards and porches that surrounded the temple proper, never to the temple building itself.

We have a good idea of what both the temple and temple complex were like, but since all of the buildings have been totally destroyed, our knowledge of these buildings depends largely on the literary descriptions in Josephus and the Talmud. We will not describe them in detail here.

THE TEMPLE COMPLEX

In the middle of the vast platform of the temple complex (about 1,500 feet by 1,000 feet) was a raised platform, 16 feet above the surrounding courtyards and paved with large stone slabs. Today in the middle of this platform stands the Islamic shrine called the Dome of the Rock or the Mosque of Omar. This mosque covers the site of the temple. In the center of the dome of the mosque there is a bare, projecting rock, the highest part of Mount Moriah, measuring 60 feet by 40 feet and standing 6 feet above the floor of the mosque.

Formerly the temple itself, the sanctuary entered only by the priests, stood over this rock. The total width of the building, including the storage chambers on the side, was about 80 feet, with a porch about 105 feet wide. The length of the building, including the porch, was about 160 feet. The base on which the building sat extended outward 15 feet on each side. The building was 150 feet high in the front.

The temple occupied only a small part of the temple platform. Immediately in front of the sanctuary was the courtyard of the priests, which contained the huge altar of sacrifice (75 feet square and 23 feet high). Only the priests could enter this area, but those for whom sacrifices were being made could observe them from porches along the entryway to this courtyard. In front of this was another courtyard surrounded by small rooms and buildings into which laypeople could enter for such activities as bringing offerings and being inspected by the priests for purity. Some of Jesus' activities in the temple complex, such as witnessing the poor woman's offering, would have occurred in this area. These inner courtyards were separated from the outer plaza by walls and porches about 60 feet high.

Surrounding these two inner courtyards—on the north, east, and south—was a large open-air plaza. The inner square of the Temple Mount, 750 feet square, which included the temple proper and the inner courts described above, was separated from the outer parts of the plaza by a fence called the soreg, which marked the area beyond which Gentiles could not go.

The rest of the outer plaza, the area outside the fence, was open to Gentiles. All around the perimeter of the outer plaza were beautiful colonnaded porches. It was in these porches and in the open plaza that most of the activities of Jesus and his disciples took place. Whether these activities took place in the open plaza or in the roofed porches depended on the weather. All of this was leveled to the ground by the Romans in A.D. 70.

Because of the Muslim control of the Temple Mount and particularly due to the fact that the Dome of the Rock is built over the temple site, this area is not at present open to archaeological excavation. Only a few traces of the temple can be detected today. On the surface of the rock within the Dome of the Rock are what appear to be traces of the foundation cuttings for the Holy of Holies. Near the top of the rock, a smooth, flat rectangle has been carved into the rock. This may have been the place where the ark of the covenant rested during the First Temple Period. In the outer plaza, some traces of steps were found that help determine the alignment of the temple courts. Until recently a few pavement stones existed that appeared to be from the time of the second temple. But the Muslim authorities seem to be taking steps to eradicate this evidence.

The only archaelogical find that can be attributed definitively to the inner portions of Herod's temple is a warning sign from the fence that blocked the Gentiles from entering into the inner part of the temple complex. This barrier, about 4 ½ feet high, was topped by signs in Greek and Latin that warned that any Gentiles who passed beyond the fence would be put to death. One of these warning signs was found during the 19th century just outside the Temple Mount. On it was the following inscription in Greek capital letters: "No stranger is to enter within the partition wall and enclosure around the sanctuary. Whoever is caught will be responsible to himself for his death, which will ensue." A portion of another of these signs was found some decades later. Recall that it was the false rumor that Paul had brought Gentiles inside this fence which led to the riot that ended Paul's last visit to the temple and ended with his arrest (Acts chapter 22).

A few small finds from the First and Second Temple Periods have been recovered from the soil dumped from Muslim excavations on the temple platform. These excavations were not proper archaeological excavations but were destructive acts without proper archaeological supervision.

Though archaeological excavation on the top of the Temple Mount is not possible, it is possible for achaeologists to investigate the outer walls of the great platform that Herod built for the temple and some of the underground areas of the Temple Mount. This investigation intensified after Israel captured East Jerusalem in the 1967 war. A more detailed report appears in appendix 3.

CHURCHES

Since the churches of Jerusalem associated with events from Jesus' ministry postdate the biblical period, they are discussed in appendix 4.

Jerusalem's Upper City

In 1948 the Jordanian army destroyed the Jewish Quarter in the southwest quadrant of the Old City and left the area in ruins. Excavations in this part of Jerusalem became possible with the Israeli capture of the city in 1967 as a result of the Six-Day War. As the quarter was being reconstructed, extensive excavations were carried out and the discoveries exceeded expectations.

For New Testament studies, the most important finds were the homes of the well-to-do in this part of the city. The home of Caiaphas and the home that Jesus borrowed for the Last Supper were very likely similar to these homes. The beautiful mosaic floors, the stone vessels and stone tables, and the fine dinnerware give us some indication of the lifestyles of the rich and famous in first century Jerusalem.

The "Herodian Quarter" excavation in the Jewish Quarter uncovered parts of six or seven houses. The houses were built on terraces, on the slope of the hill facing eastward toward the Tyropoeon Valley, providing a good view of the Temple Mount.

The Palatial Mansion is the largest, most complete, and most elaborate of the Second Temple Period dwellings uncovered in the Jewish Quarter. It provides a sample of the architecture and the splendor of the buildings typical of the Upper City. The mansion extended over three terraces with a total area of 6,400 square feet. Remains of two stories of this house were excavated. The ground floor in the western portion of the house included a central court-yard and living quarters; a basement in the eastern and northern portions included water installations, storage, and service rooms. The house had thick walls built of well-trimmed Jerusalem limestone, and its foundations were laid on bedrock. Some parts of the house were preserved to a height of 6-10 feet.

The ground floor of the elaborate western wing of the Palatial Mansion included a vestibule (entrance room) with a mosaic pavement consisting of a colored square panel with a multi-petaled rosette in the center and pomegranates at the corners. On the walls of the room next to the vestibule, frescos were preserved to a considerable height. These colored frescos are in the style popular in the Hellenistic-Roman world—colored panels, imitation marble, architectural elements, and floral motifs.

Numerous examples of colored mosaic floors were found in the houses of the Upper City, both in reception halls and baths. The decorative motifs in these mosaics include geometric designs: interlacing meanders, wavy lines, and pleated bands. Floral motifs are also common, especially stylized rosettes with differing numbers of petals. It is also noteworthy that the decorative motifs used in the mosaics and frescos of the Second Temple Period did not include representations of humans or of animals since pious Jews avoided figurative art.

Mikvehs ("places for purification," also spelled *mikva* and *mivah*) are among the most common features in the residences of the Upper City of Jerusalem. In each house there were one, two, and sometimes more mikves—evidence of the importance accorded to ritual purity. A typical mikve was cut into the rock, plastered, and roofed with a vaulted stone ceiling. A broad flight of steps led to its bottom and up again. The mikves were filled in winter with rainwater and in summer with water from the cisterns. At times bathtubs constructed of small stones, cement, and plaster were placed next to the ritual bath.

It may be assumed that the Palatial Mansion, with its location overlooking the Temple Mount and its large number of mikves, was owned by a priestly family.

THE BURNT HOUSE

The residence known as the Burnt House, located north of the Palatial Mansion, also dates from the Second Temple Period. Here evidence was found of the total destruction of the city by the Romans in the year A.D. 70. Although only a small area of the house was exposed, it proved to be richer in small finds than the other houses uncovered in the Upper City.

The ground floor of the Burnt House was exposed, revealing a small courtyard, four rooms, a kitchen, and a mikve. The walls of the house, built of stones and cement and covered with a thick white plaster, were preserved to a height of about 3 feet. Sunken into the beaten-earth floors of the rooms were the bases of round ovens made of brown clay, indicating that this wing of the house was perhaps used as a workshop. The courtyard of the house was paved with stone, and through it one reached the kitchen and the other rooms. In the corner of the kitchen were a stove, basalt grinding stones, and a large stone tray.

The Burnt House was buried under a thick layer of destruction. Throughout the house, scattered in disarray among the collapsed walls, ceilings, and material from the second story, were fragments of stone tables and many ceramic, stone, and metal vessels. This disarray is evidence of pillaging by the Roman soldiers. Leaning against a corner of one of the rooms was an iron spear, which apparently had belonged to one of the Jewish fighters who lived here. At the entrance to the side room, the arm bones of a young woman were found, the fingers clutching at the stone threshold. The many iron nails found in the ruins are all that is left of the wooden roof, the shelves, and furnishings, which were completely burnt. Numerous coins minted during the rebellion against the Romans (A.D. 66–70) attest to the date of the destruction of this house.

In one of the rooms a round stone weight, 4 inches in diameter, was found. On it, in square Aramaic script, was an inscription of Bar Kathros, indicating that it belonged to the son of a man named Kathros. The "House of Kathros" is known as a priestly family that had abused its position in the temple. A lament preserved in talmudic literature speaks of the corruption of these priests:

> Woe is me because of the House of Boethus,
> > woe is me because of their slaves.
> Woe is me because of the House of Hanan,
> > woe is me because of their incantations.
> Woe is me because of the House of Kathros,
> > woe is me because of their pens.
> Woe is me because of the House of Ishmael, son of Phiabi,
> > woe is me because of their fists.
> For they are the High Priests, and their sons are treasurers,
> > and their sons-in-law are trustees, and their servants beat
> > the people with staves.
> (Babylonian Talmud, *Pesahim* 57, I, Tosefta, *Minhot* 13, 21)

This poem aptly describes the corruption of the priesthood in the days of Christ and the apostles.

OTHER FINDS FROM THE SECOND TEMPLE PERIOD IN THE UPPER CITY

Hundreds of complete pottery vessels were found, mainly in the mikves and the cisterns of the houses where they had apparently been placed during the siege. Many of these artifacts and vessels, objects of daily use in the first century A.D., are currently displayed in the museums of the Herodian Quarter and the Burnt House.

Fragments of dozens of stone tables of two types were discovered in the excavations. Large tables of local limestone, which stood on one central leg (30 inches average height), had rectangular tabletops (averaging 33 x 18 inches) engraved on three sides with geometric and floral motifs. These heavy tables were placed against a wall.

Small, round tables, about 20 inches in diameter, made of local limestone and imported granite and marble stood on wooden tripod legs that have not been preserved. These were portable tables used for serving food to guests who reclined on low wooden couches in the elaborate reception rooms.

An enormous number of stone vessels of the Second Temple Period were found in the houses of the Upper City. The vessels were made of easily worked, soft local limestone that was found in abundance in Jerusalem. The vessels were made on a lathe or by hand. More noteworthy are the large, lathe-made vessels. They are 24 to 30 inches high with thick straight or rounded walls, goblet-shaped with wide mouths, and on a pedestal. Most of the smaller vessels are also lathe-made in a wide variety of sizes and shapes: bowls, cups, and vessels in imitation of imported pottery. Among the vessels made by hand with a broad-bladed gouge are trays and containers of various sizes. The so-called measuring cups, shaped like mugs with straight walls and large handles, were also handmade.

The stone vessel industry that flourished in Jerusalem during the first century A.D. is clearly related to the strict observance of Jewish laws governing ritual purity, according to which stone does not absorb impurity. The purity of stone vessels is also mentioned in the New Testament, in the account of the changing of water into wine at Cana (John 2:1-7).

Two fragments of light-colored plaster, dating to the Second Temple Period, were found on which a seven-branched menorah (candelabrum) is depicted. The menorah is 8 inches high and 5 inches wide. It has seven branches, with a flame on top of each branch. It stands on a tripod base and is decorated with circles separated by pairs of lines. This decoration corresponds to the biblical description of the menorah.

An important find from the Old Testament period in the Jewish Quarter is the Broad Wall, which proves that the city was extended to the Western Hill by Hezekiah's time.

Herod's Palace

In his book *The Jewish War*, the historian Josephus wrote of a "king's palace, which no tongue could describe." He was referring to the palace built in Jerusalem by Herod the Great: "A glorious palace, astoundingly beautiful, and of immense size." It was at this palace that Jesus appeared before Herod's son Herod Antipas during his trial on Good Friday. (An alternate theory is that at that time this palace was occupied by Pilate, the Roman governor.)

At present, substantial excavations of this palace are underway along the western wall of the Old City of Jerusalem, south of the Jaffa Gate. The foundations of the immense towers at the north end of this palace have long been visible, but only the lower levels from Herod's towers survive. Towers of more recent construction stand upon these foundations, the best known of them misnamed the Tower of David.

As a result of construction in the area south of the towers, new excavations are now underway in the area of the palace itself. Unfortunately, all that remains of this great palace are the foundations and the lowest levels of the walls. These lie about 10 feet below the current surface. Two massive walls were exposed, which served as a platform for the podium on which Herod's palace was constructed. Construction style of the walls is similar to other

Herodian projects in Israel: on the Temple Mount, in Caesarea, at the Herodion near Bethlehem, and in the palaces at Jericho. It is estimated that the size of the compound is about 1,500 feet long by 500 feet wide.

Most of what we know about this palace is derived from the writings of Josephus, a Jewish general in the Great Revolt against Rome (A.D. 70) who crossed over to the enemy side and lived out his days in Rome where he wrote books about the revolt. In *The Jewish War*, Josephus wrote:

A little way south of these towers and sheltered by them was the king's palace, which no tongue could describe. Its magnificence and equipment were unsurpassable, surrounded as it was on every side by a wall 45 feet high, with ornamental towers evenly spaced along it, and containing huge banqueting halls and guest rooms with 100 beds. . . . Words cannot express the varied beauty of the stones, for kinds rare everywhere else were brought together here in quantity. There were ceilings remarkable for the length of the beams and the splendor of the ornamentation, and rooms without number, no two designed alike, and all luxuriously furnished, most of their contents being of gold or silver. . . . On every side were numbers of intersecting colonnades, each differing in the design of its pillars. The open spaces between them were all green lawns, with coppices of different trees traversed by long walks [coppices are groups of trees which are repeatedly cut down to ground level and allowed to grow], which were edged with deep canals and cisterns everywhere plentifully adorned with bronze statues through which the water poured out.

Josephus also wrote that the two most beautiful rooms in the palace were called Caesarion, the room of Caesar, and Agrippion, the room of Agrippa. Josephus wrote that they were even more magnificent than the temple, Herod's greatest building in Jerusalem. Was Jesus received in one of these great rooms?

Josephus added that the palace was also intended to serve as a fortress in time of need, with the array of fortifications culminating in the three towers to the north, "which were superior in size, beauty, and strength to any in the whole world." The three towers were

- The Phasael Tower, the largest, named after Herod's brother, stood 145 feet tall;
- The Hippicus Tower, named after a friend, was 132 feet tall;
- The Mariamme Tower, named after his beloved Hasmonean wife whom he murdered, was the most ornate. Josephus said, "The king considered it appropriate that the tower named after a woman should surpass in decoration those called after men." It stood 74 feet tall.

The remains of this palace give a tiny taste of Herod's magnificent building projects, which earned him the name the Great.

Crucifixion

Despite the fact that many classical sources, including the Jewish historian Josephus, describe the crucifixion of thousands of people by the Romans, there is only a single archaeological recovery of a man crucified by the Romans from around the time of Jesus. It is not surprising that there is only one such discovery, because the crucified were usually left to decay on the cross or thrown in a dump and, therefore, would not have been preserved. The only reason these particular archaeological remains were preserved was because of the Jewish aversion to leaving bodies exposed, the same concern that played a role in Christ's burial. This crucified man was found in a tomb north of the Old City of Jerusalem, not too far from where Christ was crucified and buried.

In 1968 contractors working in Givat HaMivtar in northern Jerusalem accidentally uncovered a first century A.D. Jewish tomb. An ossuary bearing the Hebrew inscription "Yehohanan the son of Hagakol" contained the skeletal

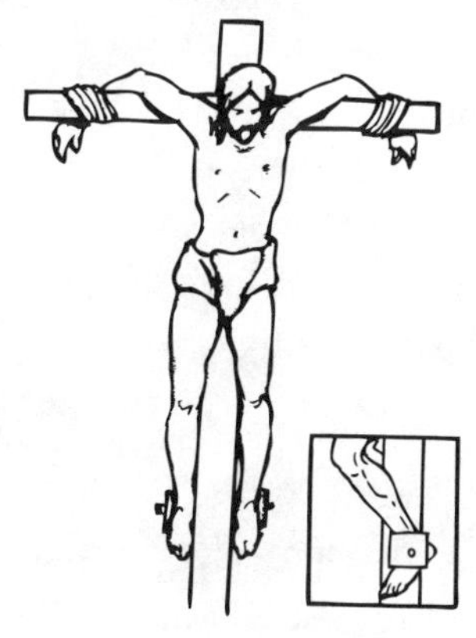

Crucifixion

remains of a man in his twenties who had been crucified. The evidence for this was the right heel bone of the individual, which was pierced by an iron nail 4 inches long. Nails were valuable and would have been salvaged, but in this case the nail had been bent, apparently by hitting a knot in the wood. Since the nail could not be extracted, the nail and the wood it was stuck in had to remain attached to the skeleton.

Pieces of wood found between the head of the nail and the heel bone suggest that prior to penetrating the heel bone, the nail was driven through a thin board to fix the leg more firmly to the side of the cross. It seems that the heels were nailed to the sides of the cross (one on the left side, one on the right side, and not with both feet together in front). The wood from the cross that remained on the nail was olive wood. Since olive trees are not very tall, it is likely that this cross was not very tall.

The victim's legs were found broken, perhaps as a means of hastening his death as described in John 19:31,32. There was no evidence of damage to the wrists, suggesting that in this case the man's arms were tied to the cross, though nailing of both hands and feet was perhaps more common. For the positioning of the nails in the hands we must depend on literary analysis, not archaeology.

In pictures of the crucifixion, Christ is shown with nails in his hands, and our translations refer to nail prints in his "hands." However, it seems that to better support the body weight on the cross, the nails would be through the wrists. The Greek word *cheir*, which is translated "hand," can refer to the hand and the forearm together. The same is true of the Hebrew word *yad*. Peter in prison wore chains on his "hands." Women wear bracelets on their "hands." In both cases, we would say "wrists."

Because there were so many methods that the Romans used in crucifixion, we cannot say too much about the manner of Christ's crucifixion, but it may be that the nail marks "in his hands and his feet" were not like those in the pictures.

Interesting articles about archaeological evidence for the ancient practice of crucifixion are Tzaferis, Vassilios, "Crucifixion—The Archaeological Evidence," *Biblical Archaeology Review 11*, February, 1985, pp. 44–53, and Zias, Joseph, "The Crucified Man From Giv'at Ha-Mivtar: A Reappraisal," *Israel Exploration Journal 35 (1)*, 1985, pp. 22–27.

Archaeological finds that can be related directly to Paul are relatively rare, but a number of the sites that he visited have substantial surviving ruins. Many of the surviving Roman structures on the sites are from later than the time of Paul, but they still give visitors a feeling of what the cities Paul visited would have looked like. There are also many pilgrim sites identified with Paul, but for the most part these are later Christian churches that, based on tradition or a guess, were built on these sites.

Syria

Neither Damascus nor Antioch in Syria have major ruins from the time of Paul. In Damascus a wide colonnaded street from Roman times is identified with Straight Street (Acts 9:11). There is also a Roman gate in the southeastern part of the Old City that is identified as the site of Paul's escape through a window in the wall (2 Corinthians 11:33).

Paul's hometown in Tarsus in Cilicia also lacks significant ancient ruins.

Cyprus

In the account of Paul's first journey, Acts chapter 13 reports a dramatic encounter between Paul and the Roman governor (or proconsul) Sergius Paulus at Paphos. This led to the governor becoming a believer. In 1877 an inscription was found near Paphos, bearing the name of the proconsul Paulus. The name of L. Sergius Paulus has also been found on an inscription in Rome, where he served as one of the keepers of the banks and channels of the Tiber in A.D. 47. This could have been after he had completed a three-year term in Cyprus. An inscription of a Sergius Paulus was also found in Antioch in Pisidia, where the Sergius Paulus' family had large holdings. Some have speculated that this is one of the reasons Paul visited Antioch shortly after his visit to Cyprus.

Asia Minor

Antioch in Pisidia has some interesting Roman ruins, particularly the Temple of Augustus, an emperor of Rome. The cult of emperor worship proved to be a particular problem for the early Christian church in general, but this was not mentioned as an issue in Paul's visit to the city.

There are impressive Greco-Roman remains at Perga, but they are from later than the time of Paul.

No major architectural remains have been found in the Galatian cities of Iconium, Lystra, and Derbe.

Ephesus is the most important and most impressive of the Pauline sites in Turkey. Ephesus is one of the most spectacular outdoor museums in the world. The site is filled with important public buildings, including temples, libraries, fountains, and gymnasiums.

The two most important buildings related to Paul's visit are the temple of Diana (Artemis) and the theater. There are scant remains of the great temple, which had been one of the wonders of the ancient world. The goddess Diana (Artemis) and her images were discussed in the chapter on idols.

The theater, on the other hand, is one of the most impressive structures in town. It seated about 24,000 and reaches a height of 100 feet. Like other ancient theaters, this theater consisted of three main sections: the skene (stage backdrop), the orchestra (place of action for the actors), and the cavea (auditorium) where the audience sat. The skene, which was approximately 60 feet high, was the most imposing section of the theater. The facade of the structure that faced the audience was three-tiered and had columns. There were statues in niches behind the columns. Elements of the theater as it stands today are from later than the time of Paul.

One of the more interesting finds is the large public latrine. This 1st-century latrine was rather advanced for its time. The 36 toilet seats, formed by cutting holes into marble benches that lined the walls of the 15 by 15 foot room, were not separated by partitions. The toilets were constructed over a channel with an uninterrupted flow of water, and they were covered by a roof. The rest of the room was open to the sky and had an impluvium (a sunken pool for catching rainwater) and fountain in the center. The floor was covered with mosaics. Supposedly, the well-to-do sent servant boys to warm up the seats for them.

Greece

The major Pauline sites in Greece are Athens and Corinth.

Athens was one of the most illustrious cities of the ancient world. In Paul's time its importance was more cultural than political. Many of the impressive ruins and reconstructions on the Acropolis (the citadel) and the Agora (the marketplace and forum) would have been seen by Paul. The most important sites for visitors today are the Parthenon and Areopagus and the Stoa of Attalus. Evidence of the idolatry that Paul encountered in Athens is preserved in the many ruins of temples and the statues of deities.

By the time of Paul, Corinth was the commercial center of the area. The city had two harbors on two seas. Cenchreae on the east connected to the Aegean and the East. Lechaion on the west connected to the Adriatic and Italy via the Gulf of Corinth. A paved roadway called the *diolkos* was used for transporting cargo across the isthmus for reloading on waiting ships on the other side. Important ruins in Corinth include the Sanctuary of Asklepsios, one of the important medical centers of the day, and the temple of Apollo or Athena. The acropolis of Corinth was the Acrocorinth, towering 1,800 feet above the city. There are many interesting ruins on the Acrocorinth and in the Roman forum. Every two years important games were held at nearby Isthmia.

According to Acts 18:12-17, Paul (in the summer of A.D. 51?) was brought before the proconsul of Achaia, Gallio, and was accused by the Jews of inciting others to "worship God in ways contrary to the law." It is very possible that Gallio judged the case from the "bema" (rostra, speaker's platform, or judgment seat), which survives in the forum. When Gallio dismissed the case, the Jews took the leader of the synagogue, Sosthenes, and beat him in front of this judgment seat. At nearby Delphi, an inscription from the time of the Emperor Claudius was discovered that says "Lucius Junios Gallio, my friend, and the proconsul of Achaia . . ." Historians date the inscription to A.D. 52, which supports the dating of Paul's visit to Corinth to A.D. 51.

Erastus, an associate of Paul in Corinth, was a financial official of Corinth. In 1928 archaeologists excavating at a Corinthian theater discovered an inscription that reads "Erastus in return for his aedileship laid the pavement at his own expense." The pavement was laid in A.D. 50. This man has been identified with Paul's friend (Romans 16:23), but the Latin term *aedile* is not identical with *oikonomos*, the Greek word used by Luke, so the two Erastuses may be different men. See the discussion in chapter 2.

Less impressive ruins are found in and around the ancient forum in Philippi, including a traditional site of Paul's imprisonment. Nearby are remains of the Via Ignatia, the ancient road traveled by Paul.

The remains of Thessalonica are buried under the modern city, but this site provides an interesting archaeological sidelight. Luke uses the Greek term *politarchs* ("rulers of the city") to refer to the leaders in Thessalonica. This was another hit against Luke's credibility for centuries because no other Greek literature used this leadership term. However, approximately 30 inscriptions have now been discovered that bear the term *politarch*, including five finds that specifically refer to the ancient leadership in Thessalonica.

Caesarea

Herod's great port of Caesarea, where Paul was imprisoned before being sent to Rome for trial, has yielded impressive ruins, which includes palaces; a Roman theater; a temple dedicated to Caesar Augustus; a hippodrome (race track) rebuilt in the second century as an amphitheater; the Tiberieum, which has a limestone block with a dedicatory inscription that is the only secular record of Pontius Pilate; a double aqueduct that brought water from springs at the foot of Mount Carmel; and the remains of the harbor.

Rome

Rome is, of course, a city with magnificent ancient ruins and many great churches. Some of the many structures around the Forum were there at the time of Paul. This site is the location of temples, basilicas, and arches too numerous to mention here. One of the basilicas there may have been the site of Paul's trial and condemnation. The Arch of Titus commemorates the destruction of Jerusalem in A.D. 70 and depicts some of the loot from the temple, most notably the menorah. In addition to the main forum, other smaller forums were located nearby.

The two sites in Rome most associated with Paul are the Mamertine Prison, where he may have been held before execution, and the second largest church in Rome after St. Peter's Basilica, the Church of St. Paul Outside the Walls, which was long believed to be his burial site.

Recently Vatican archaeologists have uncovered what they believe to be the tomb of Paul beneath the floor of the basilica. Archaeologists excavating underneath the altar uncovered a large sarcophagus with a Latin inscription *Paulo Apostolo Mart,* "Paul Apostle Martyr." The tomb dates back to at least A.D. 390. The holes through which the ancient pilgrims would have pushed pieces of cloth to touch the relic are clearly visible. The sarcophagus will be on public view, but the church has yet to rule on whether the sarcophagus will be opened.

The famous (or infamous) Coliseum postdates the life of Paul. It is an elliptical amphitheater in the center of the city of Rome, the largest ever built in the Roman Empire. It is one of the greatest works of Roman architecture and engineering. Occupying a site just east of the Roman Forum, it was built by Titus and Vespasian, the emperors who destroyed Jerusalem. It was financed at least in part by the booty from Jerusalem. Originally seating around 50,000

111

spectators, the Coliseum was used for gladiatorial contests and other public spectacles. It remained in use for nearly five hundred years. Along with the traditional gladiatorial games, many other public spectacles were held there, such as mock sea battles, animal hunts, executions, reenactments of famous battles, and perhaps the persecution of Christians.

Today many "Steps of St. Paul" tours visit these sites.

The Seven Cities of Revelation

In addition to Ephesus, which was previously discussed, of the Seven Cities of Revelation, Sardis, Pergamum, and Laodicea contain significant archaeological remains.

Important remains at Sardis are the synagogue and the gymnasium-bath complex. The synagogue is third century or later.

The Great Altar of Pergamum is now reconstructed in the Pergamon Museum of Berlin. The base of this altar remains on the upper part of the Acropolis. Tradition connects this altar, believed to be dedicated to Zeus, with John's reference to "Satan's throne" in Revelation 2:12,13.

Other notable structures still in existence on the upper part of the Acropolis include a theater with a seating capacity of ten thousand; various temples; the royal palaces; a Roman bath complex; and the library, which was one of the most important in the ancient world.

Remains at Laodicea are relatively well-preserved. Its stadium, gymnasium, and theatres (one of which is in a state of great preservation, with its seats still perfectly horizontal) are worth seeing. Among other interesting objects are the remains of an aqueduct with siphon (see chapter 4 on water systems).

Underwater archaeology has two main elements: shipwrecks and submerged ruins.

Since the 1960s, extensive underwater surveys and excavations have been conducted along the coast of Israel, with the aim of exposing remains of shipwrecks and their cargos, harbors, and other submerged structures.

Underwater archaeology should follow the same standards of measuring, recording, analysis, and publication that apply to dry land archaeology (see chapter 1 and appendix I). Naturally, it is much harder to do this underwater. Some of the excavation is done by divers. A special tool used in underwater archaeology is a type of giant vacuum that sucks up sand that is covering the wreckage or ruins. Other work is done by robots, especially in deep water.

Shipwrecks

A seagoing ship of the Persian period, the Ma'agan Michael wreck, was discovered a couple hundred feet off the coast of Israel, about 18 miles south of Haifa. Covered with a heavy layer of sand, the hull was exceptionally well-preserved from stem to stern and almost up to the waterline. It was built of pine timber with mortise-and-tenon joining, using the "shell first" mode of construction. Its bow and stern were strengthened with fiber lashings. Frames were then installed to support the structure. Also well-preserved was the ship's keel, which was made of a single beam. The vessel was originally 40-45 feet long with a displacement of 25 tons. Study of such wrecks help archaeologists reconstruct the building techniques of ancient shipbuilders.

Objects found on the vessel help reconstruct the nature of ancient maritime activities. A unique, one-armed wooden anchor was found intact at the side of the bow. Among the contents of the vessel were a set of carpenter's tools, several large storage jars, ceramic utensils, ropes, and remnants of food, as well as a heavy load of ballast stones. The ship probably foundered and was abandoned while on a commercial voyage.

Sometimes the important find is the cargo of the ship. Durable cargo like storage jars may preserve the outline and size of the ship even when the ship itself has dissolved.

In 1974, hundreds of clay figurines were found scattered along a submerged ridge off the coast north of Akko by a diver. The ship carrying this load of votive terra-cotta figurines must have sunk en route to or from a coastal sanctuary. The figurines, produced in molds ranging in size from 4 to 12 inches, represent the goddess Tinit, who stands at the top of the Punic pantheon. Her sign, a triangle with a superimposed horizontal bar and a disk, is visible on some of the figurines' pedestals. The figurines were dated to the fifth century B.C.

Sometimes a totally unexpected find turns up. The ram of a Hellenistic naval vessel was discovered in the northern bay of Atlit at a depth of 15 feet. It is cast of bronze, is about 8 feet long, and weighs almost half a ton. Encased in its rear are the bow timbers of the ship to which it was attached. The front has three protruding horizontal fins, a development from the earlier single-pointed ram. This form improved the ram's ability to shatter the enemy's hull. This ship is believed to have been built in Cyprus for King Ptolemy VI (204–184 B.C.).

The most famous ancient shipwrecks are two Late Bronze Age wrecks found off the south coast of Turkey.

The wreck of a ship archaeologists call the Uluburun, a late fourteenth century B.C. vessel, was discovered by a sponge diver in the Mediterranean Sea off the south coast of Turkey near Antalya in 1982. Using techniques of underwater excavation, archaeologists recovered its contents in eleven campaigns of 3-4 months each from 1984 to 1994.

The wreck was a merchant ship of Near Eastern, probably Cypriot or Levantine (Syrian), origin. The ship was about 50 feet long and could stow about 20 tons of cargo. The hull was badly damaged, partly by the corrosion products of the copper ingots it carried, but some parts are preserved. It was constructed of edge-joined planks of cedar (the "shell-based" method of shipbuilding)—a technique known from later Phoenician, Greek, and Roman ships. Fragments of oars have also been found. The largest piece found was 66 inches long and 2.8 inches thick.

The ship had at least 24 stone anchors on board, weighing between 260 to 460 pounds each, with two smaller ones of only 36 to 46 pounds each. Some of the anchors seem to have been spares, which also served to keep the ship balanced. Anchors of this single-hole "Uluburun type" are frequently found on the Levantine coast. A similar type was found at the Cape Gelidonya shipwreck.

Dendrochronological dating (dating by tree-ring patterns) of wood from the Uluburun ship dated parts of it to trees felled around 1400 B.C. Firewood stored aboard came from a tree felled in 1316–1305 B.C., which must have been the time of its last voyage. This date would agree well with the finds on board, for example, the Mycenaean (early Greek) pottery.

The nationality of the ship has not been determined since the articles it carried were Mycenaean, Cypriot, Canaanite, Kassite, Egyptian, and Assyrian. The ship was apparently outbound from Cyprus since it carried a shipment of copper ingots, which scientific analysis verifies were from the mines of Cyprus.

From the wealth of the cargo (more than 18,000 artifacts), it has also been suggested that the vessel may have been bound for Egypt, which was at the time a center for trade. Another opinion states that the cargo may have comprised gifts to Egyptian pharaohs. Both of these suggestions seem quite speculative. If the point of origin was Cyprus, the location suggests a voyage to the west with an international collection of goods transshipped through Cyprus.

The ship carried both raw materials, finished products, and property of the crew:

- 354 copper ingots (about 10 tons) shaped like ox hides. (It was once thought that these imitated dried ox hides as a pre-monetary form of currency, but this may simply be a utilitarian shape that makes them easier to handle and to load on the backs of horses or mules.)
- At least 40 tin ingots, which are low in lead. The source of the tin is still a matter of debate, but it might have come from

Spain (Tarshish) or from Afghanistan. These copper and tin ingots constitute the largest collection of Bronze Age ingots found on a single site.

- Unworked glass and ingots of "blue glass" for faience or glass inlay
- Egyptian ebony, for furniture
- Elephant ivory and hippopotamus ivory for furniture, inlay, plaques, etc.
- Faience vessels (earthenware covered with various glazes), ivory vessels, and a gold chalice
- Gold and silver jewelry: earrings, rings for fingers
- Amber
- Ostrich eggs
- Gold
- One ton of terebinth resin for perfumes, in Canaanite jars
- Food: acorns, almonds, figs, olives, and pomegranates
- Cypriot ring-base bowls and white slip bowls
- One large jar of carefully packed Cypriot pots
- Wide-mouthed jugs
- Clay lamps
- Large pithoi (large storage jars) probably for fresh water
- A collection of bronze tools: perhaps the equipment of the ship's carpenter
- A bronze pin with a globular head, thought to have a central European origin
- A gold scarab bearing the name of Nefertiti, wife of the pharaoh Akhenaten
- Six European-type spearheads that have parallels in the Eastern Alps and Italy
- A sword of Italian origin
- A stone ceremonial ax that comes from Bulgaria or the Carpathian Basin

The purpose of this extensive list is to illustrate the richness and diversity of trade and international contacts during the Old Testament period. In his lament for the Phoenician city of Tyre (Ezekiel chapter 27), Ezekiel provides a lively description of the international trade network of his day: the ships, the sailors, the merchants, and the commodities in which they trafficked. In his account you can almost hear and feel the hustle and bustle of an ancient harbor. The cargo list of the Uluburun ship helps us imagine the trade Ezekiel so vividly described. (Or perhaps it would be more accurate to say that the lively account of Ezekiel helps make the somewhat boring cargo list I have provided more interesting to us than it might have been otherwise.)

The second important wreck, the Cape Gelidonya wreck, was found near Finike, Turkey in 1954. Like many wreck sites in shallow water, this one was discovered by a sponge diver who stumbled on the wreck's main concentration of cargo. The wreck sat in about 85 feet of water on an irregular rocky bottom. This merchant vessel apparently ripped its bottom open on a pinnacle of rock that nears the surface of the sea. Spilling artifacts in a line as it sank, the ship eventually settled with its stern resting on a large boulder. Its bow landed on a flat, rock sea floor 150 feet or so to the north. At some point during the hull's disintegration, the stern slipped off the boulder into a natural gully formed by the boulder and the base of the island. This illustrates another point that can sometimes be determined from wreckage—the cause and manner of the sinking.

The pioneering excavation of this wreck, between the middle of June and the middle of September 1960, was the first shipwreck excavation carried to completion on the sea bed, the first directed by a diving archaeologist, and the first conducted following the standards of dry land excavation. Visits to the site in the late 1980s by a team from the Institute of Nautical Archaeology (INA) at Texas A&M University discovered more artifacts that made it possible to explain how the ship had sunk.

The excavation revealed that this was the wreck of a Phoenician merchant ship from about 1200 B.C. Among the finds were Mycenaean ceramics and copper and tin ingots. The sinking was dated to the late thirteenth century B.C. by the discovery of two nearly intact Mycenaean (period IIIB) stirrup jars and by a radiocarbon date of 1200 B.C. plus or minus 50 years from brushwood on the wreck. This brushwood dunnage made clear the purpose of the brushwood that Odysseus placed into the vessel that he had built (*Odyssey*, 5.257).

117

(Dunnage is material used in the holds of ships to protect the cargo. Brush and wood scraps were used for packing material in ancient ships.)

Because of a lack of protective sediment, most of the ship's hull had been devoured by marine borers. It is clear, however, that its planks were held together with pegged mortise-and-tenon joints, the same method of ship construction used in Greek and Roman times. The distribution of cargo on the sea floor originally led to an estimate of a hull not much longer than 35 feet, but recent discoveries suggest that this estimate is low.

The bulk of the cargo consisted of ingredients for making bronze implements, including both scrap bronze tools from Cyprus, intended to be recycled, and ingots of both copper and tin, meant to be mixed to form new bronze. The scrap, at least partly carried in wicker baskets, included broken plowshares, axes, adzes, chisels, pruning hooks, a spade, knives, and casting waste. The copper, mined on Cyprus, was shipped as 34 flat, four-handled ingots, weighing 55 pounds a piece on average. A second type was disk-shaped "bun ingots," averaging only about 8 pounds each. Other fragments chiseled from each type were also found. The tin ingots were too badly corroded to reveal an original "ox hide" shape, but seabed evidence suggests that at least one was a rectangular bar. In addition, there were 18 much smaller, flat, ovoid ingots, at least one of them bronze, that seemed to have been cast in multiples of 1.1 pounds.

The discovery on the wreck of a bronze swage (a sort of an anvil with various sizes and shapes of openings); stone hammerheads of the kinds sometimes used for metalworking; many stone polishers; a whetstone; and a large, flat, close-grained stone that could have served as an anvil suggest that a tinker/blacksmith may have been along on the voyage.

This wreck's importance derives from the historical conclusions that can be drawn from it. At the time that this wreck was excavated, it was generally accepted among scholars that Mycenaean Greeks had a monopoly on maritime commerce in the eastern Mediterranean during the latter part of the Late Bronze Age and that Phoenician sailors did not begin their great tradition of seafaring until the following Iron Age. Indeed one of the main reasons that Homer's

Odyssey has been commonly dated to the eighth century B.C. by modern classicists is his frequent mention of Phoenician sailors and bronzesmiths. This was thought to be anachronistic for a story allegedly set in the Late Bronze Age.

The Cape Gelidonya shipwreck suggests new possibilities. The southeast end of the wreck, most probably its stern, held what may be the personal possessions of the crew and/or passengers. These possessions included four scarabs and a scarab-shaped plaque, an oil lamp, stone mortars, more than 60 stone pan-balance weights (including Egyptian *qedets* and Syrian *nesefs* and *shekels*), and a merchant's cylinder seal—all apparently of Syrian, or Canaanite, origin. A razor is of Egyptian rather than Mycenaean type. There seems to be a contrast between the mostly Cypriot cargo and the shipboard mixture of Mycenaean, Cypriot, and Syrian pottery. The conclusion was that the ship was probably Canaanite (the Canaanites were Bronze Age Phoenicians). With a single exception, contemporary Egyptian artists associated the trade in four-handled copper ingots and tin ingots with Syrian merchants. After the Cape Gelidonya excavation, the only known mold for casting four-handled copper ingots was found in the port of Ugarit, the greatest of the Late Bronze Age Syrian port cities. All this suggested that Homer knew what he was talking about after all and his Phoenicians are not anachronistic in the Late Bronze Age setting of the Trojan War. The discovery in 1994 of the Cape Gelidonya ship's Syro-Canaanite or Cypriot stone anchor bolstered the contention that the ship was of Near Eastern origin. Because so many Near Eastern artifacts have been found on Cyprus from this period, the possibility remains open that the ship and crew were Cypriot. But perhaps historians were thinking too narrowly all along. The nationality of the crews of ancient ships may well have been different than the nationality of the ship's *registration* and *ownership,* to use modern terms. For further reading, this text is adapted from G. F. Bass, "Cape Gelidonya," in *Shipwrecks in the Bodrum Museum of Underwater Archaeology,* Bodrum Museum of Underwater Archaeology Publications 3, pp. 25-35. Bass is an important pioneer of underwater archaeology.

The Israelites were not much into maritime activities. When they were forced into such activities by necessity or by trade opportunites too good to pass up, they relied on a partnership with their Phoenician/Canaanite neighbors. The two wrecks we have just studied give evidence of the maritime prowess of the Phoenicians long before their commercial dealings with Solomon and Jehoshaphat and the flight of Jonah.

As noted previously, many shipwrecks in shallow water were chance finds by divers, but now systematic mapping of deep-sea wrecks is being undertaken by small robot submarines. In 1997 two shipwrecks were discovered in the Mediterranean Sea 30 miles west of Israel by the US Navy's research submarine NR-1. Further investigation in 1999 with the remotely operated Medea/Jason system found the wrecks to be from the eighth century B.C. These are the earliest known shipwrecks to be found in the deep sea. Both ships appear to be of Phoenician origin, loaded with cargos of fine wine destined for either Egypt or Carthage when they were lost in a storm on the high seas. The ships lie upright on the seafloor at a depth of 1,300 feet in a depression formed by the scour of bottom currents. The discovery of these wrecks suggests that ancient mariners often took direct routes to their destinations, even if it meant traveling beyond sight of land. This refuted the idea that ancient mariners were coast huggers who did not venture far from land.

A special case of underwater archaeology is the so-called Jesus Boat found in the Sea of Galilee. In the winter of 1986, after several years of drought, the water level of the Sea of Galilee had dropped by several meters and the shoreline had receded considerably. Two young men, walking along the shore south of Kibbutz Ginosar on the western bank of the lake, noticed the outline of a boat in the mud. Experts called in to examine the discovery concluded that the remains of an ancient boat had been found. It was decided to excavate it immediately, before the possible rise of the water level.

Innovative and sophisticated techniques were required for lifting and moving the boat. First, a massive dike was built around the site to prevent the lake from inundating it and pumps were used to keep the groundwater out. The wood had to be kept wet during the removal of the silt from inside the hull. The hull was then strengthened with fiberglass and filled with polyurethane. Tunnels were dug under the boat, and its sides were strengthened. When the extremely fragile remains of the boat were safely packed, water was pumped into the big pit that had been created during the excavation and the boat was floated to shore. It was placed in a specially built conservation pool at the museum of Kibbutz Ginosar, where the polyurethane casing was removed and the boat was resubmerged in water. In a process that took several years, synthetic wax was added to the wood to give it sufficient structural strength for display outside the pool.

The boat was found lying perpendicular to the shore, its stern toward the lake. Only the lower portion of the rounded stern was preserved. The boat's length is 27 feet. Its width is 7.5 feet and its depth 4 feet. It was built in the "shell first" fashion, with mortise-and-tenon joinery, and constructed mainly of cedar planks and oak frames. Much of the wood was in secondary use, that is, it had been recycled from older, obsolete boats. Additional wood fragments were uncovered nearby, evidence that the boat was found in a place that had served as a shipyard. The boat was large enough to carry 15 people, including a crew of five. Though apparently used for fishing, it may also have transported passengers and goods.

By the construction techniques and two pottery vessels found near it, archeologists judged that the boat was from the Roman period. Carbon 14 tests confirmed that the boat had been constructed and used between 100 B.C. and A.D. 70. It is likely that this sort of boat was used by Jesus and his disciples, many of whom were fishermen. Such boats played a large role in Jesus' life and ministry—they are mentioned 50 times in the gospels.

Nothing connects this particular boat with Jesus, but it has been nicknamed the "Jesus Boat," and larger re-creations of it ferry tourists and pilgrims across the Sea of Galilee.

Underwater Structures

Sometimes structures are underwater because they were built there in the first place (harbor installations). Others are dry-land features that are now submerged due to rising sea levels or subsidence of the land.

The most important underwater structures in Israel are at Caesarea. This large deep-water port built by Herod the Great at Caesarea

Maritima is described in detail by Flavius Josephus (*The Jewish War* I, pages 408-415). The harbor, comprised of three basins, was completed around 10 B.C. At this oldest known example of sophisticated harbor construction, survey and undersea excavations have revealed a high level of engineering technology, as well as in-depth knowledge of underwater currents and the movement of sand.

The large outer basin of the harbor was created by constructing two breakwaters to enclose a large area of open sea. An arc-shaped breakwater, more than 1,500 feet long, was built along the southern and western sides of the harbor. In the north, a shorter breakwater about 600 feet long was built westward, at right angles to the shore. Parts of the breakwaters consisted of large ashlar blocks, weighing several tons each, laid as headers on the seabed. Other portions were constructed of enormous chunks of conglomerate, cast of hydraulic cement and stone in wooden frames, sunken to the seabed. By the middle of the first century A.D., the principles of underwater construction using concrete were well known to Roman builders. The harbor of Caesarea was the earliest known example of underwater Roman concrete technology on such a large scale. The long breakwater was 130 to 180 feet wide, on which service and storage facilities were built. Its narrow, inner portion facing the harbor served as a pier for loading and unloading.

At the northern end of the long breakwater are the foundations of a structure built of particularly large blocks and preserved almost to the water level. These may be the remains of the huge lighthouse that stood at the entrance to the harbor, referred to by Josephus.

The middle basin of the harbor was smaller (720 by 660 feet) and followed the contours of a natural bay. Its loading platforms, 15 feet wide, were constructed of ashlar blocks.

The inner basin was the smallest, surrounded by the city on three sides. It had been in use in the Hellenistic period, was developed by Herod the Great, and became obsolete in the Byzantine period as a result of continuous silting.

The Caesarea harbor is the first underwater archaeological museum in the world. Divers view some 36 different signs along four marked trails in the sunken harbor, covering an area of 87,000 square yards. They are given a waterproof map that describes in detail each of the numbered sites along the way. One trail is also accessible to snorkelers. The other sites, ranging from 7 to 29 feet below the surface, are close to the beach and are appropriate for beginner divers.

Other harbor surveys were conducted at Atlit, Acco, and Dor. The sunken foundations of the Phoenician harbor at Atlit (dated to the seventh or sixth century B.C.) are believed to be the earliest known port with built breakwaters. The breakwaters were built of straight walls enclosing a natural bay. The foundations consist of large ashlar blocks laid on the rock of the seabed and along a small island offshore. A wall, which included a gate, separated the harbor from the city.

The cargos of several vessels were found at the bottom of the harbor and around it. Among them are stone anchors and large two-handled jars used for transporting wine from the Greek islands.

Perhaps the most amazing underwater find in Israel is a submerged Neolithic village near Atlit. During the Neolithic Period, the level of the Mediterranean was some 60 feet lower than it is today and the coastal plain was much wider. Some 1,200 feet off today's shore, at a depth of 25 to 35 feet, this Neolithic village was discovered under a layer of sand carried there by waves and currents, with its dwellings and artifacts well-preserved.

Twelve structures with paved courtyards and plazas between them were excavated. At the edge of the village was a long brick wall, probably for protection against winter floods, which filled the nearby wadi (dry river bed). An 18-foot-deep well cut into the sandstone, its upper part lined with stones, provided water for the village. Bronze was not yet in use during this period, so this is the earliest example of a well dug with axes and hammers of stone. Among the village houses were several stone-lined pits, 6 to 10 feet in diameter, probably used as silos for the storage of food. Fifteen tombs, some within the houses, were also found.

Many flint and bone artifacts were salvaged from the seabed, as well as stone bowls used in this pre-pottery period. Animal bones found indicate that the village's economy was based on farming, herding, hunting, and fishing.

Glacial melting following the last ice age (i.e., global warming) caused the sea level to rise, reducing the area of the coastal plain along the Mediterranean. Seepage of seawater into the wells was probably the cause for the abandonment of the village, which then became submerged.

I was not sure what to call this chapter: bogus archaeology, fake archaeology, fraudulent archaeology, biased archaeology, mythical archaeology. Finally I settled on "bad archaeology" as a catch-all phrase. Among the topics this chapter will deal with are illegal looting, forgery of artifacts, deliberate hoaxes, biased interpretations, and other types of archaeological chicanery. We can distinguish two kinds of archaeological fraud: (1) material fraud and (2) intellectual fraud. Material fraud debases the artifacts: looters destroy the context of real artifacts; counterfeiters fake or doctor artifacts. Intellectual fraud debases the interpretation of finds: biased scholars, journalists, or publicity hounds manufacture implausible interpretations of real artifacts.

Looting

Archaeology stimulates public interest in ancient objects, but it can also attract unwelcome attention from looters. A major problem for archaeology worldwide is destruction of archaeological sites by looters. Looting of archaeological sites by people in search of hoards of buried treasure was a problem already in ancient times. For instance, all but one of the tombs of the Egyptian pharaohs were looted in antiquity. Early archaeology, which often was not much more than digging for museum items, was not much better. Today the main threat is not from would-be Indiana Joneses but from illegal diggers who loot sites by night in hopes of finding ordinary objects like pots or seals to sell on the antiquities market. Tombs are especially targeted because they are the most likely source of intact items. The main loss to archaeology is not so much the artifacts themselves, since most looted items are not unique treasures, but that looters damage or destroy archaeological sites, denying archaeologists valuable information that would be recovered from controlled excavation. The artifacts are scattered and cannot be studied as an assemblage.

The demand for artifacts by collectors encourages looting and the illicit antiquities trade, which smuggles items abroad to private collectors. The looters may be poor people in Third World countries struggling to support themselves and their families, but often the looters are well-organized gangs, working with an international network of fences, smugglers, and customers. The looting problem in Israel involves both elements.

The Israel Antiquities Authority (IAA), the principal organization in Israel with responsibility for antiquities, has a computerized list of over 14,000 sites, but since 1967 more than 11,000 of these sites within the pre-1967 borders have been robbed (mostly tombs). In fact, it was looters who discovered many of these sites. The exact number of sites robbed since 1967 in the occupied territories is unknown, but it is in the thousands.

This destruction has given rise to a vehement debate within Israel between the IAA and the dealers' community and within the international archaeological community itself. The IAA wants to change the law that currently permits licensed antiquities trading. It believes that if the antiquities trade is outlawed, then dealers will no longer be able to operate in Israel and theft from archaeological sites will stop as demand dries up. The dealers, however, maintain that if such a law is passed, then the antiquities trade will simply continue underground, as happens in other Mediterranean countries where it is forbidden.

In Israel there are about 75 licensed dealers with a combined annual turnover of about $5 million. On the one hand, the sale and collecting of antiquities is allowed almost without restriction, while on the other hand, all antiquities that have been discovered in Israel since 1978 are the property of the state. Therefore, licensed, legal excavations cannot be a source of goods for antiquities dealers. Items for sale must come from existing legal collections or from illegal digging. Israel's Ministry of Tourism allows its seal of approval to be placed in the windows of the authorized antiquities shops despite the claim of the IAA that a large part of the material sold there comes from illegal excavations. While antiquities dealing in

Israel remains legal, there are certain prohibitions on the export of antiquities.

Legal dealers claim that most of their antiquities come from private collections and are purchased legally—in other words, from collections that were built up before 1978 when it was still legal to excavate on private property and to collect artifacts from the surface. It is difficult to prove otherwise since investigating the source of antiquities would make large demands on available resources. But it is hard to believe that the 100,000 artifacts that leave Israel each year all come from pre-1978 inventories.

Antiquities criminals can be divided into two groups. The first and largest group are economically depressed villagers from the West Bank and occupied territories. The IAA reports that 99 percent of the thieves are local inhabitants from villages close to the ancient sites. There are three reasons for this looting: the economic deprivation of the villagers (which is increased by the current isolation of the occupied territories), disregard for the cultural value of the antiquities, and poor law enforcement.

The second group of criminals is Israeli and foreign citizens who act as intermediaries or middlemen. They have good contacts in Palestinian villages and purchase items, often for very little money, always in cash. These antiquities are then sold to legitimate dealers who sell them to tourists or for export.

There are different types of collectors. The first group of collectors is tourists who constitute 99 percent of antiquities buyers. Many purchase a glass ornament, a jar or pot, a coin or two, or some other antiquity in one of the more than a hundred antiquities shops in Israel and the territories. In particular demand are pottery and coins, especially those associated with the Jewish Wars and the New Testament. By and large tourists do not care about where the antiquity was found. Their main interest is that the object is "old" and that it can be associated with an historic event. The items they buy are not in themselves of great archaeological or monetary value.

The second group of collectors is Israelis or foreigners who are serious collectors of big-ticket items. Some are influential public figures who have exerted pressure on the parliament not to change the current law that permits trading in antiquities. Notable among these were Teddy Kollek (former mayor of Jerusalem and chairman of the Israel Museum in Jerusalem board of directors) and Moshe Dayan (the almost legendary general and government minister who allegedly had an obsessive hunger for valuable archaeological finds). Dayan is reported to have accumulated his extensive private collection through unauthorized and unscientific digs, sometimes using Israeli soldiers and army helicopters. Most of his private collection, however, is now displayed in the Israel Museum. Other private collectors have voluntarily opened their collections to the public or to study.

Anti-market activists claim that some influential curators at the Israel Museum in Jerusalem and the Eretz Israel Museum in Tel-Aviv support the antiquities trade as it is presently constituted because it allows them to continue buying antiquities on the open market. Preventing such a trade would severely limit the museums. Antiquities displayed in Israeli museums come from both authorized and unauthorized excavations.

Big-ticket items, sold to deep-pocketed collectors, must be moved through international fences that trade in stolen and forged art of all sorts. This involves other countries besides Israel. Especially critical at the present time is the situation in Iraq, as a result of the war.

At the time of the collapse of Sadaam Hussein's regime, there was widespread looting of major museums by mobs. Most of these items were relatively unimportant items, even facsimiles from gift shops. Many of these items were recovered.

The looting of extremely valuable items was for the most part an inside job by people with knowledge, access, and connections to international dealers. Some of the major items have been recovered, but others are still missing.

A peculiar form of "looting" is that which is carried out by the Muslim authorities on the Temple Mount when they excavate for construction projects without regard for the damage this excavation may be doing to the archaeological context of this very special site. The most notorious example was excavation for an underground mosque at the southeast corner of the Temple Mount. The motive here is different from that of common looters, since the archaeological sin in this case is not greed for loot but indifference or hostility toward the temple site. Some archaeological evidence has been recovered by sifting dirt from the dumps from this digging. Legal efforts to stop this destructive digging have been unsuccessful, largely due to fear of creating a violent backlash from the Muslim population.

Regular construction anywhere in Israel could have the same destructive effect on archaeological remains if the builders conceal the discovery of antiquities in order to prevent delays or modification of the building project, but it can also be a boon to archaeology if such accidental finds are properly documented by a salvage excavation before the completion of the project. In some special cases, such as in the Jewish Quarter in Jerusalem, important finds are preserved by being incorporated into the lower levels of the building.

Forgeries

The line between looted items and forgeries is often difficult to detect, since in both cases the origin of the object is unknown. Unscrupulous collectors who buy antiquities on the black market may actually be buying fakes. Every major museum at one time or another has been victimized by fakes.

At present the most notorious controversies concerning forgery of artifacts revolve around artifacts associated with Israeli collector Oded Golan, who has been accused by Israeli authorities, together with several alleged accomplices, of forging the following artifacts:

- The James Ossuary, which bears an inscription "James, son of Joseph, brother of Jesus." It is conceded that the ossuary (bone box) is genuine but the inscription, or part of the inscription, is alleged to be a modern forgery.
- The Jehoash Inscription, which records repairs to the temple in Jerusalem, is suspected of being forged on a genuine ancient stone panel.
- An ivory pomegranate inscribed "Property of the priests of the temple" was allegedly forged on a genuine ancient piece of ivory.
- Various ostraca and seal impressions mentioning the temple or place names and personal names from the Bible.

Since the James Ossuary and the Jehoash Inscription have been subject of very sharp disagreement, which remains unresolved at the time of this writing, we will discuss them a bit more.

The James Ossuary is a bone box from the first century A.D., which bears an inscription "James, son of Joseph, brother of Jesus." James the brother of Jesus was the leader of the Jerusalem church in the book of Acts. The inscription, if authentic, would be the earliest mention of Jesus outside the New Testament and the first near-contemporary reference to Jesus in an archaeological find. It is conceded by everyone that the ossuary is genuine but the inscription or part of the inscription is alleged to be a modern forgery.

In October 2002 a press conference cohosted by the Discovery Channel and *Biblical Archaeology Review* (BAR), a high-circulation popular archaeology magazine, presented the ossuary as a major archaeological find. The find was reported in the November issue of BAR, and BAR was instrumental in arranging for the ossuary to be displayed in Toronto, Canada, during international meetings of archaeologists and Bible scholars. The authenticity of the inscription was supported by experts in 1st-century Hebrew and Aramaic epigraphy (handwriting analysis) and by scientists from the Geological Survey of Israel. But the fact that the ossuary did not come from a legitimate archaeological excavation raised suspicions. In March of 2003, the Israel Antiquities Authority appointed a committee of 14 scholars to examine this find together with the Jehoash Inscription. In 2003 the IAA announced in a press conference that the James Ossuary inscription was a forgery. To this day scientists and scholars remain divided on the authenticity of the inscription.

At first the identity of the owner was unknown, but it soon became known that it was Oded Golan, a collector with one of the most extensive sets of ancient artifacts in Israel. In March of 2003, Israeli police searched Golan's property. In July of 2003, Golan was arrested and detained. Israeli authorities claim that the search revealed a storage space rented by Golan in a Tel Aviv suburb that contained forged ancient seals and inscriptions in various stages of production, engraving tools, and labeled bags of soil from excavation sites around the country. In spite of the nature of these claims, the authorities did not hold Golan for trial but released him pending further investigation. At the time of this writing, Golan still has not been convicted of anything.

In September 2001, a then-anonymous collector brought a stone tablet with an allegedly ancient Hebrew inscription attributed to Jehoash, king of Judah, to the Geological Survey of Israel (GSI) in order to check its authenticity. The inscription described repairs made to the temple in Jerusalem by Jehoash. It corresponded to the account in 2 Kings chapter 12. Three experts from the GSI studied the tablet by various chemical and mineralogical methods. They declared the inscription to be genuine. A plausible cover story for the authenticity of the find was the suggestion that it had been turned up during Muslim excavations to create an underground mosque on the Temple Mount and that it was found in the dump from this digging. The tablet was soon linked to Oded Golan and became part of the investigation described above. In this case too the experts are divided on the authenticity of the artifact, and the legal process has not been concluded.

What should we conclude about these cases? Though the authenticity of the inscriptions may never be determined, what is very clear is the role that biases and personal interests play in archaeological interpretation. Here are a few of the biases:

- Christians would like the finds to be real since they would confirm the Bible.
- Unbelievers and skeptics are sure they must be fake because they would confirm the Bible.
- If the inscriptions are too much in agreement with the Bible, they are "too good to be true." If the style is any different from biblical Hebrew, they are "obvious fakes."
- The owner/forger could make a lot of money if the inscriptions are real but will go to jail if they are forged. If he is vindicated, the notoriety of the case will inflate their value.
- BAR has invested a lot of energy in defending the authenticity of the inscriptions.
- The IAA intensely dislikes BAR, its editor Herschel Shanks, and any finds from the antiquities market. This dislike is probably also fueled by the fact that the permit to export

the box for display in Canada was not exactly forthright in declaring the alleged importance of the inscription and the box was broken in transit.

- Some experts have gone out on a limb and now would have a hard time acknowledging their mistakes.
- Love of the limelight may keep the fires of debate burning.
- Professional rivalries may keep the fires of debate burning.
- Virtually every participant has a predetermined agenda or a vested interest in the outcome.

Heated exchanges, dueling experts, the on-again, off-again nature of the legal proceedings, press leaks from the prosecution, and the love of controversy on all sides will keep these cases in the media until the legal process is concluded—and perhaps beyond.

Repatriation

Perhaps here is the place to mention briefly the issue of repatriation. Various countries are taking action against museums, mostly in the West, to force these museums to return items that the museums purchased years ago. Some of the items are allegedly the result of illegal looting. Others were excavated or purchased under the authority of permits from the country's government at the time of purchase but under conditions that suggest colonial influence or bribery.

The governments of Italy, Greece, Turkey, and Egypt, among others, have pushed to reclaim prized artifacts from collections around the world. They have tightened their laws governing the export of antiquities or have intensified the enforcement of existing laws and international agreements. They have made impassioned public pleas on the world stage.

They have forced concessions from major museums around the world, including the J. Paul Getty Museum in Los Angeles and the Metropolitan Museum of Art in New York City. The British Museum is under persistent pressure to return the Elgin Marbles, its famous set of sculptures from the Parthenon in Athens, but it continues to resist. Resistance is based on the claim that the artifacts are safer where they are (a claim hardly deniable concerning artifacts from Iraq) and that these items are part of the cultural heritage of the whole world and should not be hoarded in one country. "What's at stake," says James Cuno, the director of the Art Institute of Chicago, "is the world's right to broad and general access to its ancient heritage." Great museums provide a unique opportunity to see the full breadth and diversity of the world's cultural history in one place.

Concerning the archaeology of Israel, the argument cuts two ways. On the one hand, important finds from Israel, such as the Siloam Inscription, are in Istanbul because they were discovered during the time when Palestine was under Turkish rule. On the other hand, the Dead Sea Scrolls, which have great interest to Israel but little interest to Palestinians, were discovered by Palestinians and purchased by Israelis at a time when Qumran was not a part of the state of Israel.

For the most part, I feel the status quo should be maintained, but any further sales should require approval of the government of the country where the artifacts are found.

Pseudo-Archaeology

Biases, preconceptions, and vested interests influence the archaeological goals and interpretations both of those who are trying to confirm the Bible and those who are trying to debunk it.

Pseudo-archaeology is the biased and unscientific interpretation of archaeological remains and sites, whether those sites are genuine or not. Archaeological frauds and hoaxes are what we might call intentional pseudo-archaeology. Extremely biased interpretation of genuine archaeological finds could be called unintentional pseudo-archaeology. When a person begins an archaeological investigation having predetermined what he wants the outcome to be, he is likely to find evidence to support his presupposition. When the perpetrator is called to answer for his spurious interpretation, he may invoke conspiracy theories in which he claims that "the Establishment," whether the scientific community or the church, is suppressing evidence (for example, *The DaVinci Code*).

NOAH'S ARK

The area of biblical archaeology that has created the most charges of pseudo-archaeology is the search for Noah's ark. From at least the time of Eusebius (died A.D. 339) to the present day, the search for the physical remains of Noah's ark has held a fascination for some Christians. Repeated "discoveries" of Noah's ark on Mount Ararat or neighboring mountain ranges have been reported, but none of them could be verified.

Ark searchers have little to guide them to the ark beyond the Genesis mention of the mountains of Ararat. The Byzantine emperor Heraclius is said to have made the trip in the seventh century. Marco Polo (died about A.D. 1324) wrote of a very high mountain in Armenia on which Noah's ark is said to have rested. But it does not appear that his group actually saw anything.

Not until the 19th century was this region of eastern Turkey safe enough and open enough to Western Christians for well-financed ark-seekers to begin exploring in earnest. Several travelers reported visiting the mountain and collecting reports about the ark.

Activity fell off in the mid-20th century during the Cold War because Ararat was near the highly sensitive Turkish/Soviet border and close to Kurdish separatist activities. Explorers were likely to find themselves in hazardous situations.

Recently the search has been largely American, supported by evangelical and millenarian churches and sustained by ongoing popular interest expressed through Christian magazines, lecture tours, videos, occasional television specials, and more recently the Internet. Former astronaut James Irwin led two expeditions to Ararat in the 1980s, was kidnapped once, and, like others, found no tangible evidence of the ark. "I've done all I possibly can," he said, "but the ark continues to elude us." The motivation of many of the searchers is summed up in this quotation from the Institute for Creation Research: "If the flood of Noah indeed wiped out the entire human race and its civilization, as the Bible teaches, then the Ark constitutes the one remaining major link to the pre-flood world. No significant artifact could ever be of greater antiquity or importance . . . [with] tremendous potential impact on the creation-evolution (including

134

theistic evolution) controversy." If only the ark were to be found, people would have to acknowledge the Bible to be true.

In 2001 the Turkish government reopened Mount Ararat to climbers. Two main sites had emerged as leading candidates for the location of the ark. The first is the so-called Ararat anomaly near the main summit of Ararat. This "anomaly" shows on some aerial and satellite images as a dark blemish on the snow and ice of the peak. The second site is Durupinar, 18 miles south of the Greater Ararat summit. The Durupinar site was heavily promoted by controversial archaeological adventurer Ron Wyatt during the 1980s and 1990s. The key feature here is a large boat-shaped formation jutting out of the earth and rock. This site is more accessible than the Great Ararat site and has received a steady stream of visitors. Some geologists have identified the Durupinar site as a natural formation, but Wyatt's Ark Discovery Institute continues to champion its claims (see the excursus starting on p. 137). Several expeditions have claimed promising results, but none of them ever produced evidence that can be examined and verified by impartial outsiders.

This lack of verification has been the trait of many widely circulated claims that the ark had been discovered. A number of individuals have reported seeing Noah's ark and even exploring it, either at the Ararat anomaly or at some other site on the mountain.

An Armenian, Georgie Hagopian, claimed to have visited the ark twice around 1908–1910 (1902 in another version of the story). Hagopian claimed that he had climbed up onto the ark and walked along its roof and that many of his young friends had also seen it. The apparent ease of getting to the ark conflicts with the accounts of other explorers. This account may be pure fiction.

Ed Davis, a US army sergeant based at Hamadan, Iran, during World War II, reported that he had climbed Mount Ararat with his driver's family in 1943. After three days of climbing, the group camped 100 feet above the ark and was able to look down into it but did not approach it closely. According to Davis' description, the ark had broken into two pieces, which had drifted some distance apart via glaciers. Its description roughly matched Hagopian's, at least judging from paintings by Elfred Lee based on Davis' descriptions.

135

David Duckworth, allegedly a volunteer with the Smithsonian, claimed to have seen photographs of the ark and crates of artifacts being unloaded from a National Geographic expedition in 1968.

All of these reports and others like them consistently fail to deliver any real evidence except the word of the discoverer. It is likely that at least some of these are complete hoaxes. These stories seem to take on a life of their own and have been circulated for decades, sometimes in variant versions. The Internet has given many of them new life. Even while compiling a summary, such as this chapter, it is very difficult to find any really credible sources.

One of the long-lived stories, which still appears on the Internet, is the story that Czar Nicholas II of Russia sent an expedition to Mount Ararat in 1917–1918 to investigate the ark. The fact that Nicholas abdicated during the February Revolution in 1917 makes the story unlikely. A few sources, apparently noticing this, put the date of the expedition at 1916. According to one version, the Russian air force was supposed to have sent 150 men to Mount Ararat in 1916 to explore a large object said to be as long as a city block, but in 1916 Russia was engaged in an increasingly desperate struggle with Germany on the Eastern Front, and it is unlikely that men and aircraft could have been spared for such an adventure. No records of such an expedition have ever come to light. The account appears to be fiction.

In 1955 French explorer Fernand Navarra reportedly found a 5-foot wooden beam on Mount Ararat some 40 feet under the Parrot Glacier on the northwest slope and well above the treeline. It is claimed that carbon 14 dating certified the wood to be about five thousand years old. Other labs have allegedly dated samples to A.D. 650 plus or minus 50 years and another to A.D. 630 plus or minus 95 years. Navarra's guide later claimed that the French explorer bought the beam from a nearby village and carried it up the mountain.

In 1977 a documentary titled *In Search of Noah's Ark* aired on numerous television stations, claiming that the ark had been found on Mount Ararat. It was based on a book of the same title by David Balsiger. This claim continues to be taken seriously by some in the ark-search community, but it is widely regarded as another hoax.

This production is not to be confused with an episode from the 1979 season of the TV series *In Search Of . . .* narrated by Leonard Nimoy of *Star Trek* fame. Earlier episodes in this program narrated by Rod Serling of *Twilight Zone* fame included "In Search of Ancient Astronauts," based on the book *Chariots of the Gods* by Erich von Daniken, and "In Search of Ancient Mysteries." The series conducted "investigations" into UFOs, Bigfoot, and the Loch Ness Monster.

In 1993 CBS aired a highly sensationalized special entitled "The Incredible Discovery of Noah's Ark," which contained a long section devoted to the claims of George Jammal, who showed what he labeled "sacred wood from the ark." Jammal's story of a dramatic mountain expedition that allegedly took the life of "his Polish friend Vladimir" was actually a deliberate hoax. Jammal, who was really an actor, later revealed that his "sacred wood" was wood taken from railroad tracks in Long Beach, California, and hardened by cooking with various sauces in an oven.

These cases pretty much typify the type of claims revolving around the ark. If there was a credible discovery, in these days of global positioning and satellite surveillance, it should be relatively easy to verify it.

One of the striking things about these pseudo-archaeology claims is the degree to which they are publicized by greedy or gullible network and cable TV channels. "Arkeology" will continue to be a staple of archaeological documentaries as long as the public buys them.

THE ARK OF THE COVENANT

The other ark, the ark of the covenant, has also been the subject of pseudo-archaeology. An ancient example is the claim of the Ethiopian Orthodox Church that the ark is in Axum, Ethiopia. Tradition maintains that it was brought to Ethiopia by Menelik I, the son of the Queen of Sheba, following a visit to his father, King Solomon. This "arkeology" lacks credibility because we know that this ark was actually put into a warehouse by Indiana Jones after he rescued it from the Nazis. (I'm being facetious.)

The most notoroius pseudo-archaeologist with a pro-Bible bias was Ronald Wyatt (died 1999). Since the WELS Question &

Answer Web site receives inquires about Wyatt fairly often, it is necessary to say a bit more about him. Wyatt had no training in the discipline of archaeology and never held a professional position in the field. His claims are dismissed by scientists, historians, biblical scholars, and most Christian leaders even in his own Seventh-day Adventist Church, but he continues to be quoted (especially on the Internet). Wyatt definitely was not a one-artifact archaeologist. He claimed to have discovered many significant biblical sites and artifacts, including the following:

- Noah's ark
- The post-flood house, grave markers, and tombs of Noah and his wife
- The location of Sodom and Gomorrah and the other cities of the plain: Zoar, Zeboim, and Admah
- Sulfur/brimstone balls from the ashen remains of Sodom and Gomorrah
- The Tower of Babel in central Turkey
- The site of the Israelites' crossing of the Red Sea, which Wyatt located in the Gulf of Aqaba, and chariot wheels and other relics of the pursuing army of Pharaoh at the bottom of this Red Sea
- The true site of the biblical Mount Sinai, located by Wyatt in Saudi Arabia
- A chamber at the end of a maze of tunnels under Jerusalem containing artifacts from Solomon's temple
- The ark of the covenant
- The original stones of the Ten Commandments (the second set)
- The true site of the crucifixion of Jesus
- The blood of Jesus, dripped onto the mercy seat of the ark of the covenant directly beneath the crucifixion site

How did all this come about? In 1960 when Wyatt was a nurse anesthetist, he saw a picture in *Life* magazine of a boatlike shape on a mountain near Mount Ararat. The resulting widespread speculation in evangelical Christian circles that this might be Noah's ark started Wyatt on his career as an amateur archaeologist. From 1977 until his death in 1999, he made over one hundred trips to the Middle East, his interests expanding to take in a wide variety of references from the Old and New Testaments. Wyatt won a devoted following among some fundamentalist Christians seeking tangible evidence of the literal truth of the Bible. But his credibility was disputed, often bitterly, by genuine archaeologists and biblical scholars. The Garden Tomb Association of Jerusalem, for example, totally denies the claim of Wyatt to have discovered the original ark of the covenant or any other biblical artifacts within the boundaries of the area known as the Garden Tomb. Archaeologist Joe Zias of the Israel Antiquities Authority has stated, "Ron Wyatt is neither an archaeologist nor has he ever carried out a legally licensed excavation in Israel or Jerusalem. In order to excavate, one must have at least a BA in archaeology, which he does not possess despite his claims to the contrary. . . . His claims fall into the category of the trash one finds in tabloids such as the *National Enquirer, Sun,* etc."

Even mainstream branches of the Evangelical movement are extremely skeptical of Wyatt's claims. "Answers in Genesis," an Evangelical apologetics ministry, has called some of Wyatt's claims fraudulent, and Seventh-day Adventist archaeolgists do not consider Wyatt's claims to be credible. Dismissed as a pseudo-archaeologist by mainstream archaeologists of every stripe, Wyatt and his followers in turn dismissed their critics as motivated by personal spite and/or anti-Christian animosity. Since Wyatt's death, some of his followers continue to promote Wyatt's research and fieldwork.

OTHER CLAIMS

Disputes about alleged biblical artifacts are nothing new. The Shroud of Turin is honored by some as the burial cloth of Christ. It contains an image of Jesus that was allegedly formed by a burst of energy at the resurrection that darkened the cloth. Critics claim that the image is a painted image of Jesus forged in the Middle Ages, but they have not given a convincing theory of how it was formed. Radiocarbon dating seemed to limit its origin to the Middle Ages, but some analysts suggest the tests were erroneously performed using samples taken from patches sewn onto the ancient cloth during the Middle Ages or contaminated from fires to which the shroud was exposed. Other analysts suggest that the dating results are skewed by limestone residue that is present on the shroud. Again, preconceptions seem to be more critical than the evidence in determining a person's stance. The form of the shroud does not correspond well with the description of Jesus' burial clothes in the gospels. This suggests they are not authentic.

A similar artifact is the Veil of Veronica, a cloth with an image of a bearded man on it. Many Catholics believe the cloth was used by Veronica (a woman not mentioned in the Bible) to wipe sweat from the face of Jesus as he walked the Via Dolorosa on the way to Calvary. This action allegedly produced a miraculous image of Christ on the cloth. Critics say it appears to be a man-made image. Viewers of Mel Gibson's *Passion of the Christ* may remember the appearance of Veronica in this movie.

At the other extreme is pseudo-archaeology of an anti-biblical bias. The gullibility of the mainstream media when it comes to pseudo-archaeology is illustrated by *National Geographic's* sensational-izing the so-called Gospel of Judas, which was trumpeted as one of the most significant archaeological discoveries in 60 years. It actually was a document already known and dismissed by the early church fathers as false and heretical.

A second example is the alleged tomb of Jesus' family in Jerusalem. Here the pseudo-archaeology was not produced by the excavator but by later populizers who sensationalized an alleged find. On February 26, 2007, a news conference was held at the New York Public Library by James Cameron, famous as the direc-tor of the movie *Titanic*, and documentary producer Simcha Jacobovici to discuss their film "The Lost Tomb of Jesus." This film discusses a tomb found in 1980 in Talpiot, a region in the south part of Jerusalem, that they claim is Jesus' family tomb. They claimed this tomb contained ossuaries with the names of Jesus, his wife Mary Magdalene, and other members of his family. Since bones are placed in an ossuary only after the body has decomposed, this find, if genuine, would refute the resurrection. They also asserted that the James ossuary discussed is a genuine ossuary from this tomb. (At the original discovery of the Talpiot Tomb, there were ten ossuaries. One, however, has since been lost.) According to the film, "recent tests conducted at the CSI Suffolk Crime lab in New York demonstrate that the patina [a chemical film encrustation on the box] from the James ossuary matches the patina from the other ossuaries in the Talpiot tomb." This documentary was presented on the Discovery Channel.

In an analysis of these claims on his own TV show, journalist Ted Koppel produced written statements from the excavator of the tomb and from the scientific organizations allegedly involved in verifying Jacobovici's claims in which they rejected Jacobovici's claims point by point. Denunciation of his claims from the archaeological community was virtually universal, coming not only from Christian archaelogists but from Jewish and secular archaeologists as well. William Dever, considered by some to be the dean of biblical archaeology in the US,* said, "I just think it's a shame the way this story is being hyped and manipulated." Similar assessments came from two Israeli scholars: Amos Kloner, who originally excavated the tomb, and Joe Zias, former curator of archaeology at the Israeli Antiquities Authority. Kloner told the *Jerusalem Post* that the documentary is "nonsense." Zias described it in an e-mail to *The Washington Post* as a "hyped-up film which is intellectually and scientifically dishonest." Dever summed up his position when he stated on Koppel's critical analysis, *The Lost Tomb of Jesus—A Critical Look*, that Jacobovici's and Cameron's "conclusions were already drawn in the beginning" of the inquiry and that their "argument goes far beyond any reasonable interpretation."

This case perhaps deserves a little closer analysis because it is a prime example of how ill-equipped the media are to deal with pseudo-archaeology and how ready mainstream media outlets are to promote it. There is virtually nothing credible about these claims, but they could thrive in the environment produced by the novel *The Da Vinci Code* (equally ridiculous in its archaeological and historical claims). Here are a few of the points that should have made it obvious to the Discovery Channel that it had a loser on its hands.

*An irony since Dever is known for his opposition to the phrase "biblical archaeology."

141

- There is nothing new: scholars have known about the ossuaries ever since 1980, and previous attempts to exploit them had failed. This is not even an inventive fraud. It is simply a rerun of an old fraud, much like the Noah's ark stories that keep circulating.
- It is not even clear if the key inscription refers to any Jesus (Yeshua), let alone to Jesus of Nazareth. The name is unclear.
- The names in question—Jesus (Yeshua = Joshua), Joseph, Maria (Mary), Matthew, and Judah—are extremely common Jewish names for that time and place.
- There is no reason whatever to equate "Mariamene e Mara" with Mary Magdalene. If this woman was a wife of one of the men in the tomb, it could have been any of them.
- Church tradition and the earliest Christian historian, Eusebius of Caesarea, report that Mary, the mother of Jesus, died in Ephesus.
- If this were Jesus' family burial site, what is Matthew doing there—if indeed "Matia" is thus to be translated?
- Why would the "Jesus Family" have a burial site in Jerusalem when Galilee was their home?
- The one member of Jesus' family who is known to have lived in Jerusalem was James, the brother of Jesus. The connection of the James ossuary with this tomb has been discredited, and the authenticity of this inscription is denied by many.
- There is no external literary or historical evidence *whatsoever* that Jesus' family was interred together in a common burial place, least of all in Jerusalem.
- This is very likely the burial site of a prominent, wealthy family from Jerusalem, not a carpenter's clan from Galilee.
- Neither of the chief perpetrators has credibility in the field. The director and narrator, Simcha Jacobovici, is serving his own speculative and financial interests. He has produced equally speculative documentaries on the exodus and the ark of the covenant. He has been called an Indiana Jones wannabe. In 2008 *TIME* and CNN reported his claims that he had been vindicated by a symposium of archaeologists. More than a dozen prominent

archaeologists signed an open letter saying these claims were completely untrue and that they, in fact, denounced his claims. As for James Cameron, how do you follow the success of *Titanic*?

- Attacks on Jacobovici's claims cannot be dismissed as pro-Christian bias. Even Israeli authorities and secular archaeologists say his claims are absurd.

Bottom line: This has been dismissed as "naked hype, baseless sensationalism, and nothing less than a media fraud, more 'junk on Jesus.'" It is a classic illustration of these axioms: "If you are looking for evidence to support your preconceived theory, you are likely to find it, whether you are a skeptic or a believer" and "It is amazing what people will believe as long as it isn't based on the Bible."

In this case, at least the perpetrators suffered the embarrasment of public exposure. At a subsequent press conference, Cameron conceded that he was not a "theologist" (I think he meant *theologian*), but he might have added that he was not an archaeologist either, nor a biblical scholarist. But a sensationalist, yes. I have not seen a similar admission of guilt on the part of Jacobovici.

The Discovery Channel seems to have come to a belated recognition that it was victimized. Departing from normal procedures, Discovery Channel didn't tout the ratings success of the program. The network also scheduled a last-minute special that harshly criticized its own documentary and yanked a planned repeat of *Tomb*. A network representative, however, insisted Discovery was not trying to bury *Tomb*.

The moral of this chapter is this: Beware of popularizations of biblical archaeology, whether they are pro- or anti-Bible and whether they appear on the Internet or on mainstream TV channels. Examine the evidence carefully and critically.

ARCHAEOLOGY AND THE DATES IN THE BIBLE

The previous chapter dealt in part with ways archaeology has been misused for the sake of profit and fame. This chapter will likewise question some archaeological claims by addressing another area where archaeology can sometimes be made to say more than the hard evidence really proves.

The question we will address is this: What can or can't archaeology tell us about early and pre-history? The problem arises when historians attempt to date archaeological finds using nonarchaeological dating methods. While this may be valid for certain time periods, this practice leads to claims that archaeology provides hard evidence for dating very ancient events or for assigning very ancient dates to sites.

To evaluate this, we will have to take a look at nonarchaeological methods of dating that are used to date archaeological sites. This chapter will help Christians come to grips with the problem concerning the time period after the flood and before Abraham.

Other Forms of Dating

Cities that have been destroyed within the well-documented periods of history can be dated by linking their destruction layers to events mentioned in historical records. For example, the destructions of Jerusalem in 586 B.C. and A.D. 70 are well-attested historically. The ruins left by those events can be clearly recognized in the excavations. But other attempts to link destruction layers with specific events mentioned in the Bible or to other records may be less certain.

Earthquake damage discovered in ruins may be connected with specific earthquakes mentioned in historical records.

Inscriptions found in their original location can date the stratum if they refer to known persons or events. The style of writing in the inscription or document can also be used as a dating tool. The coins found in a stratum can sometimes help date that level. The locus cannot be dated earlier than the latest coin in it.

Other objects that have distinct styles may be used in the same manner as pottery, for example, *fibulae* (a kind of giant safety pin used to secure clothing) or scarabs (a type of Egyptian seal). None of these methods are in themselves exact, especially if the sample is small. Results may be skewed by material from another date being mixed into the locus or when objects have been handed down as heirlooms and thus are older than the locus where they are found.

The architectural style of the buildings may also be a useful tool for dating if the buildings of a given period have a distinct style or if the masonry is cut in a distinctive way.

Scientific dating techniques, particularly carbon 14 dating, does not have great importance for most periods of biblical archaeology. Such methods can distinguish ancient finds from modern fakes and can place plant remains into their general time periods, but they are not precise enough to settle disputes about the exact dating of strata. Carbon 14 dating, which measures the decay of radioactive carbon in once-living material like wood, is being used as a cross check in some of the disputes about the early or late dating of the emergence of the kingdom of Israel, but it is doubtful that it is precise enough to give definitive answers to questions about strata from historical periods.

These dating techniques, however, become more of a factor in the chronology of early history and pre-history, which is discussed below.

The Archaeological Periods

Archaeologists have developed a standard set of names for identifying the archaeological periods in Israel. Though there are different versions of the dating chart and some dates are disputed, the following table is adequate to familiarize readers with the eras used in archaeological literature. The dating gets more precise the closer one gets to the present. The dating system derived from the

Bible places Abraham around 2000 B.C., Moses around 1400, and David about 1000.

NEOLITHIC PERIOD . . . . 8500–4300 B.C.
(pre-historic,
end of the Stone Age)

CHALCOLITHIC PERIOD . . . . 4300–3300 B.C.
(pre-historic,
Bronze/Stone Age)

BRONZE AGE . . . . 3300–1200 B.C.
(the first historical era)

Early Bronze Age I . . . . 3300–3050 B.C.
(beginning of
written history)

Early Bronze Age II-III . . . . . . 3050–2300 B.C.

Early Bronze Age IV/
Middle Bronze Age I . . . . 2300–2000 B.C.
(the patriarchs)

Middle Bronze Age IIA . . . . . . 2000–1750 B.C.
(the patriarchs)

Middle Bronze Age IIB . . . . . . 1800–1550 B.C.
(Israel in Egypt)

Late Bronze Age I-II . . . . 1550–1200 B.C.
(Exodus and Judges)

IRON AGE . . . . 1200–539 B.C.

Iron Age I . . . . 1200–1000 B.C. (Judges)

Iron Age IIA . . . . 1000–925 B.C.
(United Monarchy)

Iron Age IIB-C . . . . 925–586 B.C.
(Divided Monarchy)

Iron Age III . . . . 586–539 B.C.
(Neo-Babylonian Period)

PERSIAN PERIOD . . . . 539–333 B.C.
(Ezra, Esther, Nehemiah)

HELLENISTIC (GREEK) PERIOD . . . . 333–165 B.C.
(between the Testaments)

MACCABEAN/HASMONEAN PERIOD . . 165–63 B.C.

ROMAN PERIOD . . . . 63 B.C.–A.D. 330

    Early Roman Period . . . . 63 B.C.–A.D. 70
(Herodian Period,
New Testament Period)

    Middle Roman Period . . . . . . A.D. 70–135
(Yavne Period)

    Late Roman Period . . . . A.D. 135–200
(Mishnaic Period)

    Late Roman Period . . . . A.D. 200–330
(Talmudic Period)

BYZANTINE PERIOD . . . . A.D. 330–638
(Christian Jerusalem)

Questions About the Dating

For the first millennium B.C., the dating seems to be quite reliable, with some variations of perhaps a decade or so in the early centuries and usually only plus or minus one year in the later part of the millennium.

For the second millennium B.C., on the basis of biblical data, we have pretty solid dates for the biblical characters since we have an unbroken connection with the firm dates of the first millennium. The dating of the Egyptian pharaohs of the second millennium B.C., however, is much less certain, so we cannot simply take a chart of the pharaohs and match them up with biblical chronology. We cannot, for example, identify the pharaoh of the exodus simply by looking to see whom the history books place around 1440 B.C.

More serious questions arise in the dating before 2000 B.C. The Bible seems to allow less than three hundred years between the flood and the birth of Abraham, yet archaeology measures about six thousand years of human history that would have to be fit into this period, assuming that nothing survived from before the flood. However, only about one thousand years of this period, namely from 3300 B.C. to 2300 B.C., are based on the analysis of historical records. The rest is based on scientific dating methods, such as carbon 14 dating.

There are three ways to reconcile this discrepancy: expand the biblical chronology, compress the archaeological chronology, or through a combination of the two. Another way, of course, would simply be to reject one of the chronologies and accept the other without examining the evidence.

Questions About the Biblical Chronology

The first thing to note is that there is no actual biblical chronology for this period. The Bible uses no era for this period and gives no time intervals comparable, for example, to the reference to the time between the exodus and the temple in I Kings 6:1. What the Bible does provide in Genesis chapter 11 is a genealogy from Noah to Abraham. This genealogy gives the age of each person in the genealogy at the birth of his successor. On the basis of the not-unreasonable assumption that each man listed is the father of the man who follows him in the list, Ussher and other chronologists simply added up these numbers to produce the time interval from Noah to Abraham as about three hundred years.

More recently, prompted no doubt by archaeological and historical dating of ancient history, some evangelical scholars have questioned the validity of Ussher's assumption. It is clear that biblical genealogies can have gaps in them. Aaron's genealogy in Exodus chapter 6, David's in Ruth chapter 4, and Jesus' in Matthew chapter I all have gaps, as is clear from other sections of Scripture. Even the Genesis chapter 11 genealogy has a missing name (Cainan), which Luke, following the text of the Septuagint, includes in his repetition of the Genesis geneaology (Luke 4:36). Scholars also note the big drop in the ages of the men between Eber and Peleg, which, they say, hints at such a gap. On the basis of this hypothesis, some evangelical scholars suggest an interval of two thousand to eight thousand years between the flood and Abraham.

Though it cannot be denied that some biblical genealogies contain gaps, the biblical evidence for expanding the genealogy in Genesis chapter 11 by thousands of years is not very strong. There is no example in Scripture of such gaps in any genealogy in which the age of each "father" at the birth of his successor is given. The single example of such an omission in Genesis chapter 11, that of Cainan, may simply be a textual variant. The variant numbers in the Septuagint version of Genesis chapter 11 seem to be an attempt to provide room for more history between the flood and Abraham. So it appears the ancients were already aware of the problem.

However, we should not be too quick to try to paper over the discrepancy with this perhaps too easy solution.

The Archaeological/Historical Chronology

Beginning students of ancient history are easily impressed by the beautiful chronological charts they find in books that introduce them to ancient history. Each king or pharaoh stands magnificently in his place with the years of his reign neatly printed behind his name. However, students soon learn that reality is not so neat and simple and that these king lists are not at all like a list of the presidents of the United States, whose years in office are well-established. They find that there is not one established chronology for the ancient Near East but several competing chronologies. There are what are called high, medium, and low chronologies for both Egypt and Mesopotamia. Furthermore, for the most ancient times, these history-based chronologies must be compared with different radiocarbon chronologies, which also vary because they are based on different half-lives for carbon 14, either "uncorrected" or "corrected." However, the divergence between all of these systems is relatively minor when we are speaking in terms of thousands of years. The very debate about high, middle, and low chronologies implies that the basic framework is well-established and that our main job today is simply to tie up a few loose ends.

However, in the last century and a half, as the discipline of ancient history has developed, historians question whether the "fixed dates" of ancient history are really quite as fixed as is often implied. In the course of the development of Egyptology, the dates assigned to certain pharaohs have been lowered by more than two thousand years. The date of Sargon of Akkad has been lowered from 3800 B.C. to 2500 B.C. Hammurabi was once dated to about 2400 B.C., but the Mari records indicate that he was a contemporary of Shamshi-Adad, who is dated to about 1700 B.C.

Such drastic revisions of ancient chronology do not, of course, prove that the presently accepted chronology will be subject to the same drastic revisions as older chronologies, but they should encourage us to take a closer look at the foundations of presently accepted chronologies to try to determine if they are, in fact, much more soundly based than the older chronologies of the relatively recent past.

The fact is that there is a surprising amount of uncertainty and conjecture in the data and interpretations that form the foundation for the presently accepted chronology of the ancient Near East. We run a very real danger of debating about millimeters and centimeters, so to say, when we should rather be rechecking our measurement of the meters—that is, a great deal of effort is being spent to determine the exact days when things happened rather than focusing on the years, decades, and perhaps even the centuries that are in doubt.

Because of space constraints, we will have to limit ourselves to a check on the chronology of Egypt, which is more or less the point of reference for all chronology of the Ancient Near East. The issues in Mesopotamia, however, are quite similar.

Egypt, a Shaky Reed

There are serious questions about the validity of the foundations of ancient Egyptian chronology. The presently accepted chronology of Egypt could be in error, not just by years but by decades or even centuries. The absolute dating (that is, assigning *exact years* when events happened as opposed to simply lining up the events *in order* of when they occurred) of almost all areas of the ancient Near East is heavily dependent on matching their literature and culture with the supposedly well-established chronology of Egypt. So if Egypt is shaky, everything else is shaky as well.

One basic problem that confronts us in evaluating chronologies is that sound chronologies are based on a wide variety of fields of study. Knowledge of such varied fields as astronomy, Semitic languages, Egyptian hieroglyphics, ceramics, field archaeology, and various methods of scientific and statistical analysis are all essential factors in the construction of a dependable chronology for ancient history. Unfortunately, it is impossible for anyone to become an expert in all of these fields. To a considerable degree, a person working on the problem of chronology must depend on secondary information from disciplines in which he has very limited knowledge. This may require a person to place too much confidence in the findings of "experts" in the other disciplines, simply because one does not feel qualified to analyze or question such information. Again most of the work currently being done on ancient chronology is based on the assumption that the presently accepted chronology is built on solid foundations and that the only remaining questions concern upward or downward revisions of relatively few years. Yet the foundations themselves remain doubtful.

The following is a summary of a standard Egyptian chronology, which is based on dynasty lists and king lists and takes us to the time of Joseph, who probably went to Egypt during the 12th dynasty.

PREDYNASTIC PERIOD . . . . ca. 3500–3100 B.C.

EARLY DYNASTIC PERIOD . . . . ca. 3100–2686 B.C.

    1st Dynasty . . . . ca. 3100–2890 B.C.

    2nd Dynasty . . . . ca. 2890–2686 B.C.

OLD KINGDOM (PYRAMID AGE) . . . . ca. 2686–2181 B.C.

    3rd Dynasty . . . . ca. 2686–2613 B.C.

    4th Dynasty . . . . ca. 2613–2494 B.C.

    5th Dynasty . . . . ca. 2494–2345 B.C.

    6th Dynasty . . . . ca. 2345–2181 B.C.

FIRST INTERMEDIATE PERIOD . . . . ca. 2181–1991 B.C.

    7th/8th Dynasty . . . . ca. 2181–2173 B.C.

    9th/10th Dynasty . . . . ca. 2160–2040 B.C.

    11th Dynasty . . . . ca. 2133–1991 B.C.

MIDDLE KINGDOM . . . . ca. 2040–1786 B.C.

    11th Dynasty (note overlap) . . . . . . ca. 2040–1991 B.C.

    12th Dynasty . . . . ca. 1991–1786 B.C.

Thus Egyptian history seems to start about one thousand years before the patriarchs. There are, however, no written records for the first part of this period.

Critique of the Chronology

Although it has been made the keystone of the absolute dating of ancient history, the chronology of ancient Egypt rests on a host of unproven assumptions. Egyptian chronology rests on two pillars: on dynasty lists, which then are correlated with king lists, and on astronomical dating of key points in those king lists. There are problems with both. The following critique is rather technical but is necessary to explain this key issue in discussing the time between the flood and Abraham.

The starting point of Egyptian chronology was a dynasty list composed long after the reigns it reports. The whole structure is rendered shaky by the lateness and the fragmentary nature of the literary sources that were used for building the framework around which Egyptian chronology was built. The basic organization of Egyptian history around 31 dynasties begins with the king list of Manetho, who compiled his list in the third century B.C., three thousand years after the first reigns he records. To make matters worse, Manetho's work survives only in fragmentary quotation.

There are also severe problems with the text as it exists. It is not clear how much his dynasties may overlap with one another or how all of the royal names in Manetho's list match up with the different names recovered from ancient monuments and records. Manetho's general outline of dynasties is followed in building chronologies, but there are serious problems with his names and his sequence of pharaohs. In many cases, it is not clear why Manetho has grouped some kings into one dynasty and other kings into another. This is a very shaky beginning.

Manetho's records are supplemented and corrected by records recovered from the ancient monuments and from archaeological excavations in Egypt. The Palermo Stone from the 5th Dynasty (about 2400 B.C.) is the only major document that originates from the period preceding the 12th Dynasty, but it is only a fragment of a large slab. A fragmented papyrus of the 19th Dynasty (about 1300 B.C.), known as the Turin Royal Canon, purports to give a complete list of the kings of Dynasties 1-8, which seems to cover a period of about 955 years. But note that this source is from two thousand years after the first reigns it lists.

In many cases it is not known just how long a given king may have ruled. Comparing different publications on the history and chronology of ancient Egypt, readers may notice that a given king may be credited with a fairly short reign in one publication but a fairly long one in another.

The important point is that none of these lists provide any absolute, fixed dates for early Egyptian history since they are not linked to our modern era nor to any other system of dating that can be connected to our system. To form such connections with absolute calendar dates of our era, historians are dependent on astronomy. The primary tool for connecting early Egyptian chronology to absolute dates of our calendar is the cycle of the star Sirius/Sothis. The ability to calculate dates for early Egyptian history depends on an understanding of this astronomical cycle and must assume the consistency of the Egyptian calendar throughout the millennia in question.

Here is a brief description of the Sirius/Sothis cycle. In our calendar we add one day every four years to compensate for the fact that our earth moves around the sun approximately every 365 ¼ days. But the Egyptian calendar did not have a leap year to keep its yearly calendar and the solar year in synch. Accordingly, astronomical events, like a helical rising of a star (its reappearance in the sky after being hidden by the sun for a period of time), gradually happens at a different time of the year, moving through the calendar at a rate of ¼ day per year. This happens with the star Sirius, whose rising shifted slightly throughout the Egyptian's 365-day calendar year (as opposed to our 365¼-day calendar year). Therefore, in their calendar, the time when Sirius reappeared each year shifted ¼ of a day, passing through their whole calendar year and returning to its staring point every 1,460 years (365 x 4). This is called the Sothic cycle and is the anchor point around which the absolute chronology of Egypt in the second and third millennia B.C. has been organized. Using the Sothic cycle (as explained below), historians have dated the seventh year of Pharaoh Sesostris III of the 12th dynasty to about 1872 B.C.

Here's how historians use the Sothic cycle. Historians use 1872 B.C. (we will explain why in the next paragraph) as the starting point for *estimating* dates to Dynasties 12-20 in one direction and to the earlier dynasties of the Turin Royal Canon in the other direction. They do this on the basis of the recorded reign-lengths of *some* pharaohs and elapsed time *estimates* for some dynasties. Their reasoning progresses like this: With 1872 B.C. as a starting point, they use the list of 12th Dynasty pharaohs to calculate back to 1991 B.C. as the staring point for that dynasty. Dynasty 11 (and the contemporaneous Dynasty 10) are then traced back to 2134 B.C. in a similar way. Dynasty 9 seems to have lasted no more than 30 years, so this brings us to about 2164 B.C. The assumed 955-year span of the Turin Canon, therefore, would take us back to about 3119 B.C. as the beginning of Dynasty 1.

Since 1872 B.C. is one of the keys of all ancient chronology, we must test its validity as the anchor of the dating of early history. How was this date determined? It is based on a reference in an Egyptian document that says, "Year 7: Sothis rose helically on month four of Coming Forth (or Winter), day 16." If we know that Sothis rose helically in the 16th day of the fourth month and if we know a date when it rose on the first day of the first month (an absolute date that modern astronomy can give us), we can calculate how far the seventh year of Pharaoh Sesostris' reign was removed from the beginning of a Sothic cycle. In this way are able to establish an absolute date for the seventh year of his reign.

This sounds quite straightforward and promises an accurate absolute date on which to estimate the dates for the pharaohs and dynasties of Manetho's list and the Turin Canon. But everything is not quite so straightforward. For such dating to be valid, we must first make a number of assumptions:

- The ancient astronomical record is accurate.
- The reference in the Egyptian document has been correctly translated and interpreted by modern linguists.
- The astronomical event is a one-time occurrence that actually can be identified, so we can actually pinpoint the astronomical event that the text is describing.
- The ancient astronomical observations and records were sufficiently precise to be useful to modern astronomers for calculating the precise date of 1872 B.C.
- The event is dated in a calendar that is both precisely known and has not been changed over the years—or else we have adequate knowledge of any calendar changes so that we are able to adjust the Egyptians' calendar to ours.

Unfortunately, in the case of the text underlying the 1872 B.C. date for Sesostris, there are grounds for questioning the validity of every one of these assumptions. Accordingly, the anchor for Egyptian chronology is not dependable.

- To begin with, the text that is used to date the reign of Sesostris does not even contain the name of Sesostris. Sesostris III is associated with the text on the basis of comparing the handwriting of this text and the handwriting of other texts found at the same place that contain the name of Sesostris III.
- The Kahun Papyrus, which was the basis of this calculation, has still not been published almost 80 years after its discovery, so the opportunity to examine it has been limited to the inner circle of Egyptologists.
- There are also archaeological grounds that would lead us to take a skeptical look at this Sothic date. When this Sothic date was accepted, it became necessary to lower the date of Sesostris by over one hundred years from the date that had previously been established on the basis of the literary texts.

The discovery of Sothic dating also required considerable shortening of the time interval between the 12th and 18th Dynasties that had previously been accepted.

- Doubts about the Sothic dating of the 12th Dynasty are compounded by the fact that it does not agree with radiocarbon dating.
- The theory assumes that we have an accurate knowledge of the Egyptian use of the Sothic cycle, but we have no information from Egyptian monuments or texts that mention the use of a Sothic dating cycle in the second millennium B.C. Our information on the alleged Sothic cycle depends largely on the late classical writers Censorinus (about A.D. 238) and Theon (A.D. 379–395).
- The theory assumes there were no changes or breaks in the Egyptian calendar for over three thousand years.
- We have no certain knowledge of the date when any Sothic cycle began on the Egyptians' calendar. Theon and Censorinus give contradictory information.

From all of these problems and others not mentioned here because of constraints of space, it is clear that the foundation of Egyptian chronology is made of sand and that the early chronology of Egypt is still subject to revisions of centuries, not just decades. All the dates before the first millennium B.C. should be taken with a grain (or perhaps a block) of salt.*

Scientific Dating

We said previously that in the earliest periods of prehistory, there is a six thousand to eight thousand year discrepancy between archaeological and biblical dating. Our discussion on the interpretation of historical records has covered only the one thousand years leading up to the end of the Old Testament period. To assign absolute dates to the rest of these years, scientists rely primarily on carbon 14 dating.

*For a fuller treatment, see John Brug, "The Astronomical Dating of Ancient History Before 700," Wisconsin Lutheran Seminary, online essay file.

What is the premise of carbon 14 dating? Living plants take in carbon. A portion of that carbon is radioactive carbon 14. When a tree dies, it stops taking in carbon. Radioactive carbon decays and returns to its natural state; specifically, in about 5,700 years, half of the radioactive carbon in the wood should have disappeared. Therefore, a piece of wood that contains only half as much radioactive carbon as we would find in a living tree should be about 5,700 years old.

The method sounds pretty simple. But it is only as valid as its basic assumption, namely, that trees growing ten thousand years ago took in carbon 14 at the same rate as living trees today. If this assumption is wrong, the entire system is invalid. For example, if the store of radiocarbon in the atmosphere has varied greatly during various periods of history—due to such factors as fluctuation of radiation from space, industrialization, atmospheric nuclear testing, the burning of fossil fuels, etc.—the method will not work. There are also problems with contradictory results and with scientists being selective in what data they use.

We don't have the space in this book to examine carbon 14 dating in detail. But the following quotation reveals that even within the scientific world, carbon 14 is viewed as problematic. It was only *partly* tongue-in-cheek when a scientist at a Nobel symposium on scientific dating said, "If a C^{14} date supports a theory, put it in the main text. If it doesn't entirely contradict it, put it in a footnote. If it is completely 'out of date,' we drop it."

Conclusion

As we noted at the beginning of this chapter, we have three options when we attempt to reconcile the biblical dates of the period between the flood and Abraham with current secular scholarship. We can expand the biblical chronology and claim there are thousands of years between the flood and Abraham; we can compress the archaeological chronology; or we can construct a combination of the two.

There are ample reasons to be skeptical about the reliability of astronomical and scientific dating of early history. It may be possible, merely on the basis of questionable historical or scientific dating techniques, to substantially compress the six thousand to eight thousand years of discrepancy. On the other hand, it is difficult to envision being able to compress all the pre-patriarchal history into the few centuries of Ussher's chronology. And as we noted previously, it is possible that on the basis of Scripture, the biblical chronology can be expanded from the three centuries one gets by adding up the figures in Genesis chapter 11.

However, there is no biblical or archaeological evidence to demonstrate that we *must* do this. While it is possible to suggest various theories that would combine Genesis chapter 11 with modern interpretations of archaeological data and reconcile the discrepancy, there is not enough firm evidence at the present time to prove any of them.

Archaeology can do much to help us understand life in biblical times, and in doing so, it can help provide us with a better understanding of biblical stories. To a limited degree it also provides corroboration of biblical events and persons. We must, however, remember its limitations. It operates with only a small part of the evidence, and that evidence must be interpreted. Biases for and against the Bible often come into play in that interpretation.

In regard to the topic of this chapter and to all the topics covered in this book, we conclude that archaeology is a helpful but limited tool for understanding the text of the Bible. We should not make archaeology more or less than it is.

Archaeological evidence and interpretation cannot help us with the deeper spiritual meaning of biblical events. That comes only through the divine illumination of the Holy Spirit.

THE METHOD USED IN ARCHAEOLOGICAL RESEARCH

To carry out a successful archaeological project, an archaeologist (or more likely a team of archaeologists) needs various resources. He or she needs a site to excavate; a set of goals for the excavation; a plan for the excavation; permission to excavate the site; a support staff of supervisors, workers, and researchers; and enough money to fund the project. It is important to understand this process in order to be aware of the limitations of archaeological conclusions based on limited evidence.

Finding a Site

Sometimes archaeologists have a site thrust upon them. If construction of a new building turns up potentially valuable archaeological remains, the construction cannot proceed until the finds have been investigated and recorded. In some cases, if the material is important enough, the project may even have to come to a halt until a means of preserving the finds has been established. If archaeological materials are appearing on the antiquities market and the police are able to trace the looted items back to their source, an emergency excavation must be undertaken to save the remains that are still intact in the ground. Looting destroys much of the archaeological value of the objects that it uncovers because it rips them out of their context, which is necessary to understand their significance (see chapter 12 on bad archaeology). A salvage excavation may be able to recover some of that context by carefully excavating the parts of the site not yet damaged by the looters or construction workers. Most salvage excavations are conducted by archaeologists who are employed by the government's antiquities authority. Some salvage excavations may grow into full-fledged excavations if the site is of special importance.

Most full-fledged excavations, however, are the carefully planned projects of an archaeologist or team of archaeologists who choose a specific site that will fit in with their research interests. They choose a site that is likely to produce results from the time periods in which they have special interest, or they may return to a previously excavated site to seek answers to unresolved questions or controversies about the site.

Until recently most archaeology in Israel focused on the excavation of the ruins of cities and towns. Because cities were often built on more easily defended high points and because the mud-brick and stone construction of ancient cities produced thick accumulations of debris as the city was destroyed and rebuilt many times over the centuries, the ancient remains may sometimes be many meters thick. These urban sites are often large mounds called tells (also spelled tels). *Tell* is an Arabic/Hebrew word meaning "a mound of ruins."

Such tells are easy to find since they stick out from the landscape like sore thumbs. Many of them actually look quite similar to the large, landscaped mounds of garbage that one finds near many large American cities as waste disposal sites.

If the ancient name of the site is known, the archaeologist can determine something about the history of the occupation of the site from the written records of the city's past. Pottery scattered on the surface of the tell or washed out by erosion also gives some evidence of the periods in which the site was occupied. If archaeologists hope to concentrate their work on periods from the distant past, the preference is a site without a lot of more recent material piled on top of the periods they hope to reach. (You can't just bulldoze away the later stuff to get to the earlier stuff you really want.) In some cases remains of ancient walls or other structures may be visible on the surface. Crop marks and various types of ground-penetrating radars may also help locate the most promising sites for excavation. Excavators are especially interested in large public buildings that might have written records.

Smaller sites like villages, farms, or camps may be located by surveys conducted on foot. Aerial photography and satellite imagery may help locate sites. Underwater sites, such as shipwrecks, may be located by submarine survey. Chance finds by divers in the sea or by farmers on land may also alert archaeologists to sites.

Using all these sources of information, an archaeologist has a good chance to choose a site that fits his or her interests, abilities, and resources.

Identifying Sites

Once a tell has been discovered, chosen for excavation, and mapped, how is it identified with a specific biblical city? Some sites like Jerusalem, Bethlehem, and Nazareth have been continuously occupied since biblical times, so their identities are no mystery. But what happens when such information is not available?

There are about 475 places named in the Bible. Of these, the identities of about 280 are fairly well established. Many ancient lists of sites name places that are neighbors to one another. If the identities of several places in the vicinity are established, by process of elimination we may be able to identify the remaining sites. If I know from written records that there were three cities close to one another named x, y, and z, and if I can identify two cities as x and y, I can suggest with a high degree of probability that the third not yet identified city is z. There are many surviving ancient lists of groups of neighboring cities—from the Bible, from rabbinic literature, from military campaigns, and from pilgrim journals. These itineraries often list the order in which travelers visited a series of cities. They may describe the geographic setting of the city. They may even give the mileage between cities. If we know the location of some of the cities in a list, we may be able to use the information in the lists to identify the tells that lie between the known cities. In some rare cases, the identifications made in this way may later be confirmed by written evidence found on the site, such as boundary markers, monuments, or economic documents. For example, markings on jar handles from the city of Gibeon confirmed the identity of the site.

Most often, however, the identifications of cities that were not continuously occupied were made through the Arabic place-names of the sites today. The charting of these place-names was done by explorers of the 19th century. This study of place-names is called toponomy. In many cases these Arabic names preserve remnants of the ancient Hebrew name or, more rarely, of the Greek name. Ain Shems preserves the ancient name Beth Shemesh. Beit Lahm is Bethlehem. Taffuh is Tappuach. Wadi Yabis identifies the locality of Jabesh. El Gib is Gibeon. There are fairly regular patterns in the way in which Hebrew letters mutated into Arabic.

In a few cases, the Arabic name is a translation of the Hebrew name. Arabic *El Qadi* and Hebrew *Dan* both mean "judge." In most cases the Latin and Greek names of places in Israel were ephemeral and it was the Semitic names that endured, but a few Greek names carried over into Arabic. At the site of ancient Schechem, Neapolis ("new city" in Greek) became Nablus in Arabic.

Choosing a Site

Given the hundreds of sites available to be excavated, why might an archaeologist choose a specific site? There are many factors that might play a role.

- One factor might be the fame or the potential of the site. Many would love to excavate in Jerusalem or Jericho, but the chances of being given an opportunity are slim.
- Does the archaeologist have enough prestige to gain a permit to get the site he or she wants?
- Many archaeologists have a special interest in certain time periods. A person interested in the time of the judges (the Late Bronze Age) would prefer a site that had evidence of remains from that period but also was largely abandoned after that time period so that he would have easy access to the levels he was interested in.
- A person interested in the Philistines would love to work at a city in their Pentapolis, their five chief cities.
- A site might be chosen to solve a specific research need. For example, if a large tell in a region was being excavated, small nearby sites would be desirable to complete the regional

162

picture. Size and prestige of the site are less important to archaeologists today since many are interested in studying everyday life and are not necessarily expecting to find major historical data.

- If the interpretations of the data from a previous excavation at a site had started a controversy, an excavator might want to return to the site seeking new evidence to resolve the dispute.
- A chance find at the site might raise hopes of great finds. For example, if pieces of cuneiform tablets were found at a site, hopes of finding a library or archive would boost the appeal of the site (this is a factor in the renewed excavations at Hazor).
- Accessibility and availability of a site would also be factors. Do contemporary villages or cemeteries cover the site? Is it in a remote region?
- What are working conditions like at the site? In Israel and the occupied territories today, security at the site becomes a factor. How safe is the area?

Starting an Excavation

Major steps of an excavation are (1) finding a site; (2) researching the history and the potential of the site, including any previous excavations or surveys; (3) getting permission to excavate; (4) raising enough money to carry out the excavation; (5) assembling a staff and obtaining equipment and accommodations; (6) scouting and surveying the site and developing a plan of attack; (7) carrying out a number of seasons of careful digging; (8) keeping very accurate records; (9) preservation, restoration, and analysis of the material; and finally, (10) publication of the results.

We have already discussed points 1 and 2 in the preceding section. The necessary permissions include negotiations with any landowners and obtaining an excavation permit from the government. Fundraising may include the need to seek grants from individuals or foundations or from the local community, as well as support from one's own institution. Most American excavations in Israel today are partnerships between Israeli schools of archaeology and American universities, colleges, and seminaries. The staff consists of a director or co-directors; area supervisors (some of whom may be graduate students); specialists, such as pottery restorers, photographers, metallurgists, botanists, and linguists if there are written records. Much of the actual digging in contemporary excavations in Israel is done by volunteers who pay their own way. Many of these are students, but others are laypeople with an interest in archaeology. Support facilities, such as dormitories and dining facilities, and support staff, such as cooks and bus or van drivers, must also be arranged. After much labor and planning, the excavation is ready to begin.

The Excavation

Since only a small part of the tell can be excavated, after the necessary clearing of the ground of brush and grass, excavation begins at a number of places on the tell. These places are chosen because of their potential for major finds, like city gates or public buildings, or to obtain a sample of the strata in various areas of the tell. Often a large deep cut may be made of one place on the tell to get a preliminary idea of the different eras that are represented at the tell.

Since archaeology is not a treasure hunt or a rummaging through of the tell looking for beautiful or salable objects but an attempt to reconstruct the history of the site, very careful record keeping is of utmost importance. Archaeological finds _have_ little value if they cannot be placed into their context. Records must indicate the exact find-spot of every object and of every observable architectural and geological feature.

Before the excavation begins, the tell has been carefully surveyed and marked. The horizontal dimension of the tell is controlled by a grid of 5-meter squares. Each square on the tell has its own name or number. Every horizontal point on the tell can be identified by its location in a given square. All around the tell, the surveyor has marked a number of points on which the precise elevation has been recorded. Using these as points of reference, every vertical point on the tell can be identified with a specific elevation. In the past these measurements were taken with levels and meter sticks. Now much measuring is electronic.

As the excavation proceeds, each square is divided into locations called *loci. Locus* is the Latin word for "place." A locus is any identifiable unit. It may be a pit or a layer with a certain color or hardness of soil. It may be a room. All the items on one floor would be in one locus. Items beneath that floor on a lower floor would be in a different locus. Different rooms on the same level would be different loci. A change in the color or hardness of the dirt would lead to a new locus number being assigned. All items found in a given locus are placed in buckets (later in storage bags) tagged with the number of the locus. All of the dimensions of the locus are carefully recorded.

Initially, loci are arbitrary units of excavation whose meaning is not yet clear. For example, two parts of the same room may lie in adjacent squares, so items from the same room may initially be in different loci, including even pieces of the same broken pot. Later, as the excavation proceeds, the relationship of the loci will hopefully become clear so that loci can be combined into meaningful units.

One of the goals of the excavation is to recognize and distinguish the various layers of the city that are piled on top of one another, like layers of a cake. The archaeologist wants to be able to tell which items belong to the city from the tenth century B.C. and which items come from the eleventh century B.C. city below it. Each layer of the tell is called a *stratum* (plural *strata*). The tenth century B.C. city may be called Stratum 7 or VII if it is the seventh layer from the top of the tell. The eleventh century B.C. below then would be Level 8, and so on.

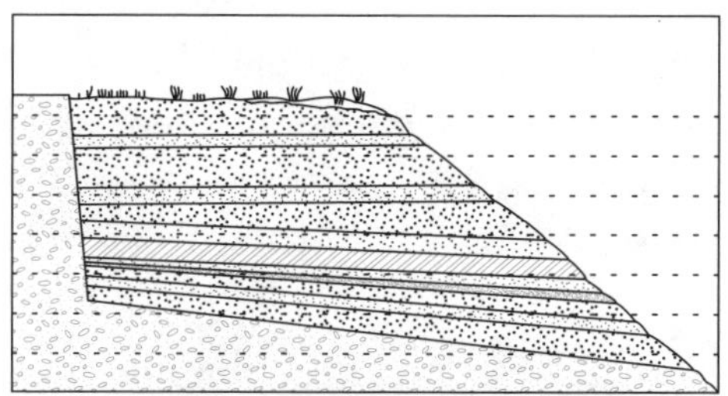

Strata (Layers) of a Tell

All of this sounds much simpler and more accurate than it really is. Rather than being like a beautifully layered wedding cake sitting on a table, the tell is like a cake that has been dropped on the floor. Each layer of the cake has been squashed flat. Layers are

165

broken and mixed together. Kids have been sticking their fingers into the frosting and nibbling bites of the cake. In most strata, all that is left are the stone foundations and beaten floors of the buildings and the stuff that was smashed on the floor at the time of the destruction. Some of the walls have been cut through by later construction. Stones have been robbed for later construction. Erosion may have transported material from its proper locus to another. Pits may have been cut through floors, placing material from one time period onto the floor of an earlier time period. Floors are often paper-thin layers of white lime that are easily missed by the excavator, with the result that items from what should be two loci are mixed together. Strata are easily recognized when they are distinct in color and hardness, as when two levels of hard brown dirt are separated by a layer of fine gray ash. But unlike the bright, clear strata of layered jello, the successive constructions of cities may all be the same color of mud-brick.

The archaeologist tries to produce some order out of this chaos in a number of ways. The first is careful excavation. "Digging" is somewhat of a misnomer for what goes on in the excavation in a mud-brick city. It is more like scraping than digging. A shallow layer of the dirt is scraped into a bucket with a tool that resembles a large hoe. Any items found in the dirt are placed in properly labeled buckets. The dirt is removed and dumped (sometimes it is sifted for small finds like beads or bone fragments). If the dirt is really hard, it may be necessary to break it with a pick, but this must be done carefully. The excavator must be careful not to dig through one layer into another. Digging around more delicate objects will be done with a small handpick and a trowel. Skeletons may be excavated with dental tools, paint brushes, and air blowers.

A second safeguard is careful record keeping. Every locus must be mapped. Careful photographs or drawings must be made of every architectural feature. Any changes in the color or hardness of the dirt must be noted. A special form of record preservation is the balk. A *balk* is a wall of dirt that is left standing on all four sides of each square. The surface must be kept clean and flush so that it looks almost like a real wall. Especially when the surface of the balk is dampened with a mist of water, one can see the strata in the balk.

If one suspects that the dividing line between strata has been missed, sometimes the missing floor can be found in the balk when it is torn down. Sometimes a paper-thin floor that was missed can be found by a careful digging touch. If one is scraping or pulling small layers very carefully from the balk, the pieces may break off right at the floor level and then one can see the white lime on the bottom of the piece. Before the balk is torn down, a drawing and photographic record must be made of it so that some record remains for later reference. Archaeology is destruction. The portion of the site that is excavated is destroyed. That is one reason that records are so crucial for later scholars who want to study the site.

In the chapter on pottery, we discussed how loci and strata are dated using pottery typology.

Exceptionally well-preserved or unique features, such as mosaic floors, wine presses, or clearly outlined buildings, may be preserved or even restored as part of an archaeological park that can be viewed by the public. Important finds, such as restorable vessels, metal objects, or idols, are preserved in museums or study collections. The most important form of preservation is publication. An archaeologist who destroys a site by excavating it has a moral obligation to publish the data in a form in which it can be studied by later researchers. In past decades, full publication was often neglected as archaeologists moved from one site to another without putting in the necessary time at the study desk. Governmental and scholarly agencies and sponsors of digs are now exerting more pressure on excavators to publish detailed final reports in a timely fashion.

Though this appendix may be somewhat tedious to the non-specialist, it is important as it illustrates the complexity of archaeological evidence and the uncertainty and subjectivity of conclusions based on that evidence, all of which bears on the reliability of the archaeological insights proposed for the study of Scripture.

Life on the Tell

Since much of the digging in archaeological excavations in Israel today is done by volunteers, it would be relatively easy for you, the reader, to arrange to spend a couple of weeks or a couple of months digging at an excavation in Israel. It does not take any particular expertise since on-the-job training is provided. Anyone with the ability to do moderate to heavy physical labor and the willingness to contribute the time and the money can participate.

Until the relatively recent past, many expeditions lived in tent camps at the site with relatively primitive facilities. This still may be done in remote areas, but more recent expeditions in Israel have been housed in dormitories or hostels and commute daily to the site. A typical schedule is to rise before sunrise to beat the heat of the day, grab a quick mini-breakfast, hurry to the site (sort of like a normal school or work day), get a few hours of work in during the cool of the early morning, eat a hearty onsite breakfast in the middle of the work day around 9 A.M., get back to work for a few more hours till noon or I P.M., head back to quarters for lunch, nap or rest in the early afternoon, in the late afternoon do pottery washing and sorting, then have supper, and finally go early to bed if you are wise (many are not). Some expeditions provide afternoon or evening lectures and weekend field trips. This is a factor to consider when choosing a site. Location on a beach, not in a desert, is another desirable attribute of a camp.

Archaeology and Music in the Bible

How great it would be to have a recording of David's performance of his psalms or a CD of a liturgical service by the temple orchestra on one of the great feast days such as Passover or Pentecost! But, of course, what we have left from these ancient musical performances is only the sound of silence. The only surviving evidence that we have of the music of ancient Israel is the written documents that explain ancient musical theory, the pictures of musical instruments, and a few surviving instruments recovered by archaeologists.

Musical Theory

It is clear from archaeological finds that the art of music was much more highly developed at a much earlier date than some people have supposed. The decipherment of cuneiform tablets from the city of Ugarit in Syria has revealed that musical notation and the use of harmony in singing were known in the Syria-Palestine cultural sphere four hundred years before the time of David. Musical texts from the Sumerian and Babyonian cultures of Mesopotamia are available from even earlier. These texts describe seven heptatonic and diatonic scales. These correspond to Greek modes or tunings, such as Dorian, Phrygian, Lydian, etc. One Hurrian song from Ugarit, which is apparently a hymn to the moon goddess, seems to have been written in a scale like our modern major scale (its Akkadian name is the "fall in the middle scale," and it is equivalent to the "Lydian tuning" of the Greeks).

If this decipherment is correct, it appears that the peoples of the Ancient Near East used a seven-note scale that closely resembles our do-re-mi scale. The seven scales used in the tuning of ancient stringed instruments were similar to the seven scales that can be played on a piano with no black notes. Each scale would begin on one of the seven notes (C, D, E, F, G, A, B). Each scale would be different, because without the black notes, the half steps would come in different places within each scale. We do not know how many of these principles of musical theory were understood and used by David and his musicians, but they were known in their time. David may have been a natural musician who played by ear, but it is likely that the Levites would have been trained in musical theory in professional schools of music.

It is interesting to note that the hymn from Ugarit discussed in the preceding paragraph had a footer that listed the composer, the copyist, and the scale to be used. This parallels the type of information provided in the psalm headings. The musical notations also include a list of intervals (string pairs) and numbers. There do not seem to be any directions for rhythm or tempo. There is still some dispute about the interpretation of all these notations since translation of ancient musical terms depends in part on applying our contemporary musical theory to ancient texts.

The Musical Notation of the Psalms

The Masoretic Text of the Old Testament is marked with two complicated systems of "accents" (*ta'amim* in Hebrew). One system of signs is used in the poetic books—Psalms, Job, and Proverbs. The other system is used in all the remaining books of the Old Testament. In addition to providing punctuation and accents, these marks provide the directions for how to chant the words of the text.

In a loose sense, the effort to decipher these signs in order to get as close as possible to the original music of the psalms is an archaeological undertaking. The problem is that the musical value of these signs has continued to evolve so that today the individual signs have different musical value in different parts of Jewish tradition. It is not likely that these signs preserve the music of the first temple, but they may derive from the music of the second temple or the early synagogue. The present interpretation of the signs by various groups of Jews gives us a starting point for interpretation. The Hebrew names of the signs give some help with efforts to interpret them. One sign, for example, is named ascending and descending. Another is called chain.

Archaeology provides a few clues. Observers wonder why some of the marks are above the letters and some are below. In ancient times music was sometimes transmitted to the musicians by an elaborate system of hand signals called cheironomy. This type of directing is portrayed in Egyptian wall paintings.

System of Hand Signals (Cheironomy). From *The Music of the Bible Revealed* by Suzanne Haik Vantoura, translated by Dennis Weber. Reprinted with permission.

It has been suggested that the marks in the biblical text are placed above and below the text as a way of representing the upper and lower hands of the director. We have to concede, however, that archaeology does not give us enough help to confidently reconstruct the original music of the Bible.

The Musical Instruments of the Psalms

The area in which archaeology gives us the most help is in visualizing and reproducing the musical instruments mentioned in the Bible.

During public worship in the temple, the singing of the psalms was accompanied by a musical group that we would call an orchestra, since it consisted primarily of stringed instruments. David's orchestra on the occasion of the ark being brought into Jerusalem included 3 cymbal players and 14 players of stringed instruments (1 Chronicles 15:19-21). The average orchestra was probably 12 to 36 stringed instruments. Apparently, other types of instruments referred to in

Psalms and the many other instruments referred to in the rabbinic writings were used only outside of the temple worship proper, primarily for festival processions.

Our knowledge of the sound quality of the instruments used to accompany the psalms is limited. Very few examples of such ancient instruments have been preserved intact, and those stringed instruments that have been partially preserved generally lack the strings, so we are unsure of what material should be used to reconstruct them, which, of course, influences the sound. Quite a few ancient pictures, carvings, and descriptions of such instruments have survived, so we do have a good idea of what they looked like.

Numerous attempts have been made to reconstruct the ancient instruments, and recordings of such instruments are readily available on the Internet.

STRINGED INSTRUMENTS

The most important instruments in the music of the temple were the stringed instruments. The two chief instruments were the *kinnor* and the *nebal.*

The stringed instrument played by David was the *kinnor.* This has traditionally been translated "harp," but the translation "lyre" is more appropriate (see following). The kinnor was smaller than our modern harp but was similar to it in some respects. Like our harp, it had an angular shape and a sound box at the bottom. *Kinneret,* the Hebrew name of the Sea of Galilee, may mean "Harp Lake." The angular shape of the lake approximates the shape of the kinnor.

The number of strings on such a lyre varied from 3 to 22, but 7 and 12 were the most common numbers. The strings were probably made of sheep gut. At Solomon's time the frames were made of almug wood (perhaps sandalwood) (1 Kings 10:11,12). At other

Lyre of Ma'adanah the Daughter of the King Jerusalem 7th century

Israelite Lyre Player Lachish 700 B.C.

Canaanite Lyre Player Megiddo 1200 B.C.

times, frames may have been made of metal. The kinnor could be played either with the fingers or with a plectrum or pick.

The Greek translation of *kinnor*, however, is not "lyre" but "cithara," from which our word *guitar* is derived. The Greek cithara apparently had a triangular shape and seven strings. The Greek lyre may have been a *U*-shaped instrument or an instrument with a tortoiseshell sound box, but we do not know the exact difference between the lyre and the cithara.

The kinnor was widely used in the Ancient Near East well before the time of the psalms (see Genesis 4:21). It was used for both secular and religious purposes. The root *knr* also occurs in several of the other Semitic languages as the name of a musical instrument. A number of pictures of ancient lyres have been found by archaeologists. A selection of these lyres is reproduced here. The first lyre pictured is from a seal that belonged to Ma'adanah, a daughter of one of the kings of Judah about three hundred years after the time of David (some suspect this seal is a fake). The Megiddo lyre and the Lachish lyre, which belonged to an Israelite musician captured by the Assyrian King Sennacherib, are closest in time and place to the kinnor of David.

The *nebel* was probably a larger version of the kinnor. It may also have produced a lower tone. According to most authorities, it had more numerous and thicker strings than the kinnor. Though the term *nbl* can refer to a water skin, there is no evidence that the nebel was like a bagpipe. One suggestion is that the kinnor provided the melody line and the nebel provided a deeper base line. Large, "floor-model" harps are pictured in Egyptian paintings, but the nebel was probably more portable. The NIV appropriately translates *nebel* as "harp" in Psalm 150:3 and several other passages. A 10-stringed nebel is mentioned in Psalms 33:2; 92:3; 144:9. (Unfortunately the NIV has also translated *nebel* as "lyre" and *kinnor* as "harp" in these three passages, the exact opposite of its better translations in Psalm 150:3. Thus the NIV fails to distinguish these two instruments consistently.)

Comment on harps and lyres: We can sympathize with the NIV's difficulties with the terms *harp* and *lyre* since the correlation between ancient and modern musical instruments is not exact. When refer-

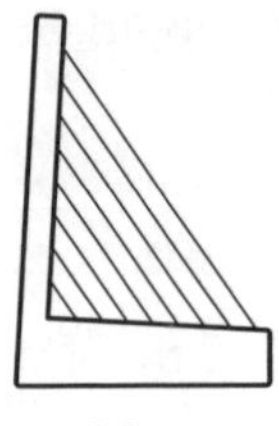

Harp

ring to ancient stringed instruments, most musicologists use the word *harp* to refer to an instrument shaped like a bow that has been filled with other strings inside the bowstring. A sound box is attached to the outside of the bow. Harps may also be angular in shape as on the left, or they may be triangular with a wooden frame that goes around all three sides of the strings. Such "harps" may be either handheld or large floor models.

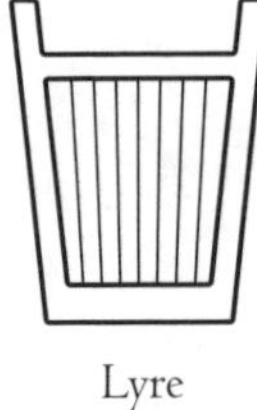

Lyre

A lyre consists of a sound box with an aperture on the side and two upright arms spanned by a crosspiece. The crosspiece may be at an angle so that different length strings may be attached to it, or it may be parallel to the top of the sound box so that all strings are the same length. Strings may be parallel to one another or in a fan shape.

In short, lyres are basically four-sided stringed instruments while harps are three-sided.

On the basis of this technical definition, the Greek *lyra, cithara,* and *psalterion* would all be classified as types of lyres. Since the *lyra* sometimes used a small tortoise shell as its sound box and the *cithara* was a more elaborate, decorated wooden instrument, *cithara* would be the best Greek translation for *kinnor.* Both the kinnor and nebel apparently were types of lyres, so "little lyre" and "big lyre" would probably be the best English translations. But since this sounds awkward, maybe we will have to settle for "lyre" and "harp."

WIND INSTRUMENTS

Shophar is sometimes translated "trumpet" by the NIV (Psalm 150:3), but at other times it is more correctly translated "ram's horn" (1 Chronicles 15:28; Psalm 98:6). In later times a shophar could be made of metal, but it retained the shape of a ram's horn. The shophar was valued for its loud and far-sounding tones (Exodus 19:16,19; 20:18; Isaiah 58:1). In the temple it was used to signal the arrival of feasts and holy days. The priests blew the shophar at the new moon and full moon, on the feast of the new year (Psalm 81:3), and to proclaim the Year of Jubilee (Leviticus 25:9). The shophar apparently was also used for making "trumpet blasts" or fanfares within services.

The *chatzotzarah* was a straight metal trumpet without valves. It was probably high-pitched. In Psalm 98:6 the NIV translates *chatzotzarah* as "trumpet." The blasts of the trumpets, blown by priests only, were used not in the instrumental accompaniment of the music of the service but primarily for signaling. In some respects their function was similar to that of church bells, which may be rung at the beginning and end of the service and at key points like the Lord's Prayer. At certain points in the service, the trumpet served the same function as the fanfare that announced the arrival of the king in ancient times (or of the president today). At times the trumpet blasts may have been a signal to bow before the Lord. According to rabbinic traditions concerning the second temple, even the posture of the performers showed this distinction of function, for while the Levites who

Ram's Horn

Metal Trumpet

were performing the liturgy stood facing toward the sanctuary, the priests with their silver trumpets faced in the opposite direction, toward the people.

The *chalil* was a flute or pipe of some sort. Some think it was a reed instrument like a clarinet or oboe. For sacred use it was more often made of wood than of metal. It apparently was thought of as a more secular instrument, and therefore, it did not have a prominent role in the temple worship proper. However, it could be used in the popular celebration of sacred festivals. The flute was also used by the festive pilgrim bands on their journey to Jerusalem to accompany the Songs of Ascents that were sung on such occasions (Isaiah 30:29). It was also customary to play it at marriage feasts and at funerals (Matthew 9:23).

The *ugav* is a mystery. The main suggestions are some sort of flute or pipes or some sort of instrument similar to a bagpipe. The NIV has "flute" in Psalm 150:4. Some older versions translate *ugavas* "organ." According to the Talmud, there was a kind of

Flutes

organ (the *magrephah*) used in the second temple, but whether it was merely used for giving signals or for accompaniment cannot be determined. The Talmud in some places describes *ugav* as a hydraulic organ of some sort, but in other passages it is treated as a flute. A long flute seems to be the best guess.

PERCUSSION

The *tof* is a small handheld frame drum, similar to a tambourine in size and shape but without the metal rattlers. It was apparently used for processions and festive dances outside the temple (1 Chronicles 13:8) rather than for choral music inside the temple. It is mentioned three times in the psalms (Psalms 81:2; 149:3; and 150:4). Other types of rattles or noisemakers were apparently used along with the *tof.* In 2 Samuel 6:5 the term *sistrum* refers to such a rattle or noisemaker.

Two types of cymbals were an important part of the temple orchestra. In fact, the three most famous Levitical musicians— Asaph, Heman, and Ethan—were all cymbal players (1 Chronicles

Tof

15:19). One source suggests that in the second temple only the orchestra leader played the cymbals. Perhaps the cymbals played a role in laying down the tempo or beat, much as the drums often do in a modern band, but some claim they were used only to signal the start of the music or of another portion of the service. The precise difference between the two kinds of cymbals mentioned in Psalm 150 is not known. The "cymbals of hearing or attention" may have been smaller and more high-pitched than the "cymbals of acclamation." The first may have been struck lightly in a horizontal position and the second struck more forcefully in a vertical position. Most surviving examples are rather small, 3 or 4 inches, but Josephus speaks of large bronze instruments. It is probable that few of the large cymbals survive because the metal was recycled.

Though archaeology can help us picture the temple orchestra and the festive processions to the temple, it cannot recover the sound for us. We will have to wait for heaven for that.

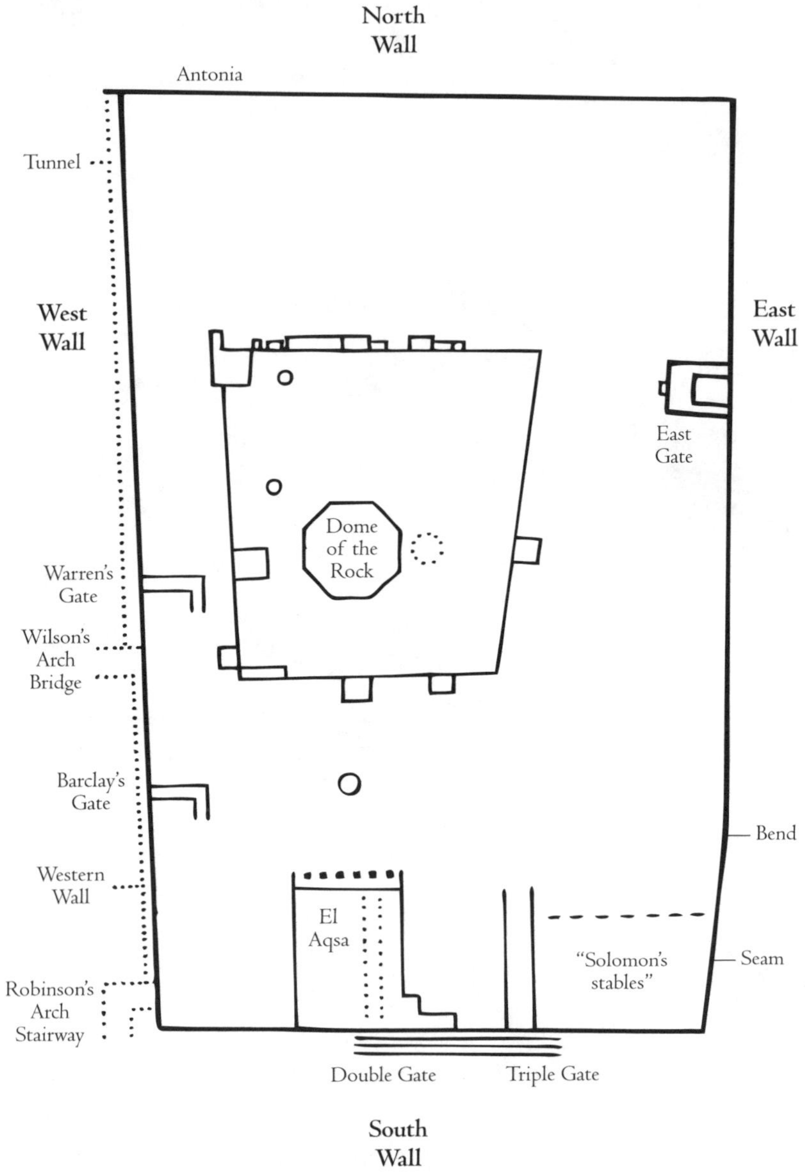

The Temple Platform

The Temple
in Jerusalem

In this appendix we will give a more detailed account of the excavations around the perimeter of the New Testament temple.

The Temple Platform

The dimensions of the trapezoidal temple platform are 1,591 feet on the west, 1,542 feet on the east, 1,033 feet on the north, and 918 feet on the south. This covers an area of about 35 acres.

THE NORTH WALL

Along the north wall of the temple complex, the ground level of the platform is about the same as that of the city outside its boundary. Today this whole area is covered with buildings, so no systematic excavation is possible. The rock on which the Antonia fortress was built is visible from the north court of the temple. This rock is topped by some Herodian stones that are very likely from the Antonia fortress, which this book accepts as the site of Jesus' trial before Pilate and the arrest of Paul.

THE EAST WALL

Along the eastern wall, archaeological possibilities are also limited by present circumstances. Deep rubble from the temple complex lies all along the outer face of the wall, but it cannot be excavated because a Muslim cemetery lies on top of the rubble. Nevertheless, there have been two interesting finds along the eastern wall.

The East Gate into the temple is now blocked. The structure of the gate as it is seen above ground today is a late Islamic construction, but underground, beneath this Islamic gate, there are remains that may be from the gate of Herod's time. Traces of this gate have twice been photographed due to a collapse of the ground next to it (or due to illegal digging, depending on whom you believe). The floor of this ancient gate was below the level of the temple plaza, and entry was by steps.

Closer to the south end of the eastern wall the ground level drops rapidly and portions of the Herodian wall are exposed. Here observers can detect the boundaries of the two southern expansions of the temple platform. A bend in the line of the wall indicates where the Hasmoneans began to expand the mount southward. Farther south the difference between the stonework of the Hasmonean and Herodian sections is very apparent at the seam that divides these two sections.

THE SOUTH WALL

The south wall is the most exciting. Since 1967 this area has been cleared of rubble all the way down to the Herodian street level. Along the street at the base of the Temple Mount one can see the outlines of the shops that were burned when the Romans destroyed Jerusalem. Black burn marks show where the arches of these shops stood. Recent archeological digs have found many miqvas ("ceremonial baths") for the ritual purification of the worshipers. Broken stones from the beautiful porch that stood on the southern edge of the temple complex were found piled on this street. These stones include decorative elements from the porch and an inscription marking the place on the roof of the porch where

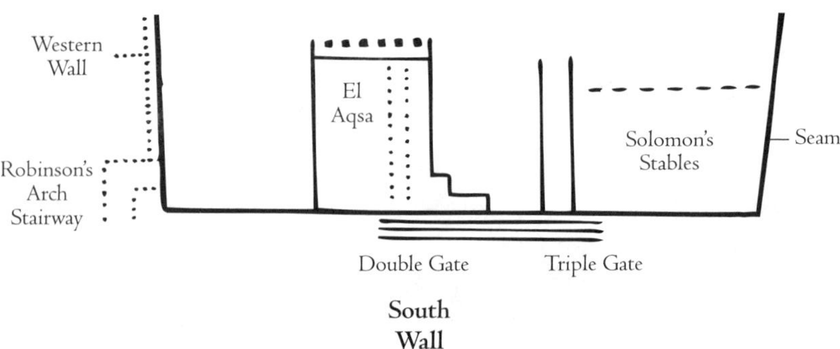

**The Temple Platform:
South Wall**

the priests stood to blow the trumpets. The grand stairway, more than 200 feet wide, which worshipers ascended to reach the underground tunnels leading to the temple platform above, has been cleared and restored. The entrances to the tunnels are visible but are now blocked, so no entry is possible.

Three groups of gates (all sealed) may be seen in the southern wall. The Single Gate, 100 feet from the southeast corner, probably dates from the Crusader period and was repaired by later Muslim rulers. The Triple Gate, about 275 feet from the southeast corner, was apparently an entrance for the temple staff. The Double Gate, farther west, south of the El-Aqsa mosque, was the main entrance for worshipers entering from the south. During the Second Temple Period, these two sets of gates divided the Temple Mount into three almost equal sections. The interior of these gates and their openings onto the Temple Mount have long been closed to visitors by the Muslims. More detail on these gates follows on page 183.

The Southern Extension of the Temple Mount

The Temple Mount (also called Mount Moriah) is a fairly level plateau at its northern end, but it slopes down sharply toward its southern end. It was Herod's plan that the entire mountain be turned into a level platform, doubling the usable area. To do this, a trench was dug around the mountain and huge stone blocks were laid in the trench. The largest stone block measures 45 feet by 11 feet by 15 feet and weighs around 600 tons. Most were in the range of 2.5 by 3.5 by 15 feet. Average weight was 5 or 6 tons. The thickness of this wall is up to 15 feet. This stone retaining wall was raised to a height that permitted the entire mountain to become one level platform.

The southern wall of this platform, where the height of the platform above the surrounding ground level is greatest, is over 900 feet long. The wall as it stands today preserves evidence of five periods of construction and reconstruction. The lower courses are the original Herodian stones, with the characteristic fine dressing, double margin, and slightly prominent smooth boss in the center. Next are large blocks, smoothly dressed, apparently dating to Aelia Capitolina, the Roman construction in A.D. 132. These are topped by smaller, smooth stones, alternating with discs (cross sections of columns inserted into the wall) which are probably late Islamic. This section is interspersed with small blocks having very prominent bosses and margins, apparently Crusader (about A.D. 1100). The final courses are small stones of later periods. The wall at the southwestern corner was about 120 feet high. The courses of the southern wall of the Temple Mount range from 3 to 5 feet in height. The 28th course from the foundation is known as the "grand course." It is almost 6 feet high and runs from the southeastern corner to the Double Gate on the same level as the gate thresholds.

The problem Herod faced was especially severe at the southeastern corner of the platform. In this area the bedrock slopes down steeply toward the Kidron stream, and a very high wall was needed to create a level platform. Herod filled in only the lower part of the space behind the retaining wall with dirt. It would have been impossible to continue this method to the top of the wall. The weight of the earth would have collapsed the wall outward. To prevent this, on the lower, leveled area he had constructed, Herod built several levels of vaults and pillars that supported the southeastern court of the Temple Mount platform. The building of these arches created underground halls, some of which later came to be known (incorrectly) as "Solomon's Stables." The size of these "stables" is approximately 90 feet from east to west and 180 feet from south to north (other sources give larger dimensions). Their height is an estimated 27 feet. The present structure of the "stables" is not the original Herodian work but later rebuilding. During the time of the second temple, these probably served as storage areas. The Muslim authorities have recently been excavating in this area to convert the area into an underground mosque. This activity is extremely controversial, since it may be damaging archaeological remains.

In this area, the total height of the retaining wall was more than 150 feet. It is suggested by some that this southeast corner is the pinnacle of the temple to which Satan took Jesus during his temptation. (Others suggest it was the southwest corner, the place of the blowing of the trumpets.) However, due to the reburial of the lower courses of the wall already at the time of construction and the buildup of rubble, only a small portion of the southeastern corner of the wall stands above the rubble today.

According to Josephus, this formidable structure made the temple into a mighty fortress, unequaled in the architecture of antiquity. He wrote (*Antiquities* XV, 11), "This wall was itself the most prodigious work that was ever heard of by man."

The Gates in the Southern Wall

THE DOUBLE GATE

The Double Gate, now walled up, was the main entry into the temple from the south. In front of this gate was a street with shops next to the gate. A grand stairway, more that 200 feet wide, approaches the gate. Ritual baths in the area gave worshipers a place for cleansing before they entered the temple. Some believe that this is the Beautiful Gate mentioned in Acts chapter 3.

Worshipers entering or leaving the temple from the south passed through these gates, one of which was in-bound, the other out-bound. This entry lies below the level of the plaza of the temple. Worshipers proceeded through underground passages that passed below the Great Stoa until they reached the western Huldah Gate through the southern wall of the first temple, where they ascended by steps to the plaza. The name Huldah may derive from the prophetess Huldah, who was believed to be buried nearby. But the Hebrew word *huldah* means "mole," an animal that tunnels underground, so some believe it refers to the tunnel through which worshipers passed to reach steps that ascended to the temple courtyard. This does not seem likely, since when the Huldah Gates were first built, they were not approached by a tunnel.

Today the outer face of the Double Gate is largely concealed by a later building, The gate is about 40 feet wide and is divided in two by a large pillar. Each doorway is 18 feet wide and 36 feet high. The southern gates of the Temple Mount were walled up after Saladin's conquest of Jerusalem in 1187.

The inner face of Double Gate can be approached from within the Temple Mount courtyard from the northeast corner of the El-Aqsa mosque. Sixteen steps and a double gallery lead down to a hall whose ceiling is supported by a row of gigantic pillars. From here one can see the inner face of the Double Gate in the southern wall of the Temple Mount. Beautiful Herodian decoration is still visible in the ceiling domes. Visitors are not normally allowed to enter these passages. When I was living in Jerusalem, our group from the archaeological institute had obtained permission to tour these underground passages, but when the Muslim custodians realized that there were Jews in the group, they "could not find the key." There are some fears that the Herodian work here may be destroyed.

THE TRIPLE GATE

Further east is the Triple Gate, an entry used mainly by the temple staff. This gate provided easy access to the underground passages and rooms in the area of "Solomon's Stables." The entire width of this gateway (51 feet) can be seen in the southern wall of the Temple Mount. This passage led to the eastern Huldah Gate through the wall of the first temple. Part of the west doorpost remains from the original second temple structure. The thresholds of both the Double and the Triple Gates lie about 40 feet below the present level of the courtyard. The Triple Gate received its present form during the Crusader period.

Other underground passages reach further into the Temple Mount. Their inaccessibility continues to fire the imagination of treasure seekers.

There are contradictory measurements on some of the features of the Temple Mount, so the figures above should be regarded as approximations.

The Western Wall

Here by the term *western wall*, we refer to the entire western wall of the temple complex, which is nearly 1,600 feet long.

The name Western Wall, however, is also applied to the small section of the western wall formerly known as the Wailing Wall, which was and is the main area of Jewish worship at the Temple Mount today. This "Western Wall" is an exposed section of the ancient retaining wall situated on the western side of the Temple Mount. It is about 190 feet long. This section faces a large plaza and is set aside for prayer. At the Western Wall Plaza, the total height of the wall from its foundation is estimated at 105 feet, with the exposed section standing approximately 62 feet high. The first seven visible layers are from the Herodian period. This section of wall is built from enormous stones, most of them weighing between two and eight tons each. Each of these stones is surrounded by fine-chiseled borders. In the Herodian period, the upper 30 feet of the wall served as the outer wall of the double colonnade along the western edge of the plaza. This upper section was decorated with pilasters, the remainder of which were destroyed at the beginning of the seventh century when the Byzantines reconquered Jerusalem from the Persians and their Jewish allies. Today the upper levels of the wall are later repairs, mostly from various Islamic periods, but with some additions as late as 1967.

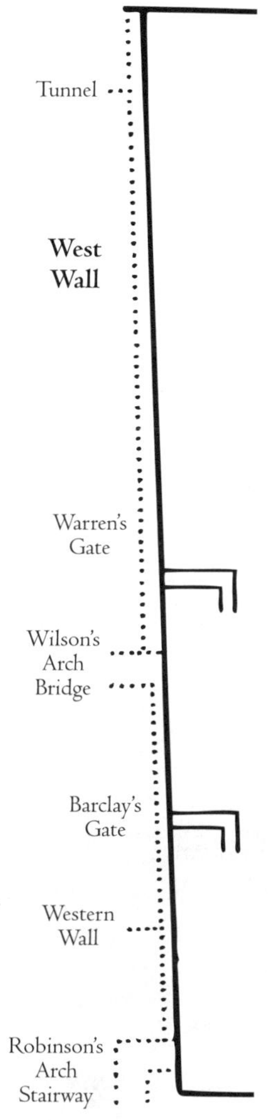

**The Temple Platform:
West Wall**

The western wall, however, is much more than the Western Wall in the narrow sense. It stretches for 1,600 feet, most of which is hidden under residential structures built along the northern portion of the wall. We will look at some of the other features along the western wall from south to north. These features are usually named after the explorers who first mapped or charted them during the 1900s.

ROBINSON'S ARCH

Until 1967 much of the area south, from the Wailing Wall to the southwest corner of the mountain, was buried under rubble from the temple. Just above ground level, 40 feet from the southwest corner of the Mount, the stub of an arch was visible. Since 1967 excavations have cleared this rubble down to the level of the Herodian street below. This stub was thought to be the remains of the last arch of a bridge leading to the temple from the western hill. Excavations have revealed that this was really the top of a monumental staircase, 50 feet wide, which took worshipers into the western end of the Royal or Great Stoa (porch). After passing over the large arch, the staircase turned to the south and descended over a series of five or six smaller arches to the street level about 60 feet below.

This staircase crossed over a Herodian street and shops that ran all along the western wall of the temple. Like the southern street, this street too was covered with rubble from the temple.

BARCLAY'S GATE

Barclay's Gate lies at the southern end of the Western Wall (in the narrow sense). Only a part of its upper lintel is visible today. This stone is almost 7 feet high. It is approximately 25 feet long. The gate was about 29 feet high and 18 feet wide. This gateway was reached by steps that came up from the street. After passing through the gate, worshipers ascended to the plaza on an *L*-shaped staircase.

WILSON'S ARCH

At the north edge of the Western Wall Plaza is Wilson's Arch, the largest arch of the Great Bridge that linked the Upper City to the west with the Temple Mount on the east. The area under the arch today serves as the inner, covered section of the Western Wall Plaza. The present form of the arch is a reconstruction from the Muslim period.

Josephus called the valley at the foot of the western wall the Tyropoeon Valley (Greek for Valley of the Cheese Maker). In those days, since the valley was deeper, it was difficult to go directly from the Upper City to the Temple Mount without crossing the Great Bridge, which also supported the last leg of the aqueduct that brought water from Solomon's Pools in the Judean Hills to Jerusalem and the Temple Mount.

Based on the information we possess, it is impossible to determine the exact dimensions of the bridge during the Second Temple Period. It was apparently destroyed by Jewish rebels at the beginning of the Great Revolt against the Romans in an attempt to prevent the Romans from getting from the Temple Mount into the Upper City. The arches were reconstructed in the early Muslim or perhaps the Roman period.

WARREN'S GATE

In the Western Wall tunnels, visitors can see Warren's Gate. In the Second Temple Period, this gate led from the street that Herod built along the Western Wall to an underground passageway that connected to the Temple Mount Plaza via a flight of stairs. It is similar to Barclay's Gate. It is 18 feet wide and 35 feet tall.

THE WESTERN WALL TUNNELS

After the Six-Day War, the Ministry of Religious Affairs of Israel began an excavation aimed at exposing the full length of the western wall by tunneling along the wall from Wilson's Arch to the northwest corner. The excavations lasted almost 20 years and revealed many previously unknown facts about the history and geography of the Temple Mount. The tunnel exposes the total length of the wall, which was previously hidden below ground, revealing the methods of construction and the various activities carried on along this wall. It is clear that the entire western wall is Herodian construction. Warren's Gate lies about 150 feet into the tunnel. Its sealed-off entrance has been turned into a small synagogue known as "The Cave," since it is the closest point a Jew can get to the Holy of Holies, assuming it was located at the traditional site under the Dome of the Rock.

The biggest stone in the western wall, sometimes called the Huge Stone or simply the Western Stone, lies within the tunnel and ranks as one of the heaviest objects ever lifted by human beings without powered machinery. The stone has a length of 40 feet and an estimated width of between 4 and 15 feet. Estimates place its weight at 570 tons. It may serve the function of providing stability in earthquakes.

Originally tourists traveling from south to north through the tunnel had to make a U-turn and retrace their steps back to the entrance. In 1996 a new exit was cut through from the Struthion Pool area at the northern end of the tunnel to the nearby Via Dolorosa. Palestinian leader Yasser Arafat used this event to incite violence, alleging the real aim was to make the Haram al-Sharif (the Muslim name for the Temple Mount) collapse (an absurd claim since the tunnel follows the outside of the western wall and does not go under the Temple Mount). Riots erupted in which 70 Palestinians and 16 Israeli soldiers were killed. Since then it has been possible for large numbers of tourists to enter the tunnel's southern entrance near the Western Wall, walk the tunnel's length with a tour guide, and exit from the northern end.*

*Books on the Temple Mount include: Leen Ritmeyer, *The Quest, Revealing the Temple Mount in Jerusalem*, Jerusalem: Carta, 2006—Extremely detailed study of the temple with great pictures. Highly recommended. Leen and Kathleen Ritmeyer, *Secrets of the Temple Mount*, Washington, DC: Biblical Archaeological Society, 1998—Much briefer. Eilat Mazar, *The Complete Guide to the Temple Mount Excavations*, Jerusalem: Shoham Academica Research, 2002. Many Web sites, such as "The Western Wall," have a lot of data and virtual tours. Use with caution. Some sites have their own agenda.

CHURCHES
OF JERUSALEM

There are many churches in Jerusalem associated with events of Jesus' ministry, but the connections are based in tradition. For that reason they lie outside the sphere of biblical archaeology in the narrow sense. We will mention only a few of the most interesting.

All Nations

The Church of All Nations in the Kidron Valley below the East Gate of the temple is a modern Roman Catholic church built over the traditional rock of Gethsemane. The remains of older churches lie below it, but there is no archaeological evidence that can be specifically linked to Gethsemane.

Gallicantu

The Church of Saint Peter in Gallicantu was built in 1931 on the eastern slopes of the western hill of Jerusalem, now known as Mount Zion, to mark the traditional site of Caiaphas' palace and to commemorate Peter's triple denial of Jesus and his tears of repentance. *Galli-cantu* means "rooster-crow" in Latin. There is evidence that a palatial home occupied the site. According to tradition, Jesus was imprisoned in one of the underground rock-cut chambers or cisterns below this mansion.

More interesting are nearby stone steps that have been dated to the time of Christ. This ancient flight of steps, sometimes called the Macabbee Steps, can be seen in the garden of Gallicantu. What is unusual about these steps is that they are very possibly the steps on which Jesus walked when he was brought up from Gethsemane. In many areas of Jerusalem, the street level of Jesus' day is well below the present street level due to the accumulation of centuries of debris, so pilgrims walk above the streets of Jesus' day, not on them.

Flagellation

The Church of the Flagellation (whipping) at the eastern end of the Via Dolorosa has no particular archaeological interest. It is identified with the Antonia Fortress at the northwest corner of the Temple Mount, where Pilate had Jesus whipped. The most interesting archaeological find in the area is the pavement, far below street level, under the nearby Convent of the Sisters of Zion.

This pavement has been identified with Gabbatha. *Gabbatha* is the Aramaic name of a plaza in Jerusalem that is also referred to by the Greek name *Lithostrotos.* The name occurs only once in the Bible, in John 19:13, where it states that Pontius Pilate brought Jesus forth and sat down in the judgment seat, in the place that is called *Lithostrotos,* in Hebrew *Gabbatha.* After descending through the basement, past a large cistern, one comes to the street level of Roman times. There one finds the paving of a Roman courtyard. Among the graffiti scratched on the pavement is a game played by the legionnaires, the Game of the King.

Also in the area is the Ecco Homo (Behold the Man) Arch. Part of it can be seen at the street level of the Via Dolorosa.

All of this would make a great connection with Christ standing in the arch of Pilate's courtroom, near the pavement where the mocking soldiers stood. Unfortunately, it seems that all of this construction is from the time of the Second Jewish War, a century after Christ.

Via Dolorosa

The Via Dolorosa (Latin for "Way of Sorrow") starts from the Church of the Flagellation. This street (really a set of streets) is traditionally believed to be the route that Jesus walked on the way to Calvary. Nine of the fourteen Stations of the Cross are on this street. (The last five stations are inside the Church of the Holy Sepulchre and will be briefly mentioned in that section.) This street is one of the main sites for Christian pilgrims to Jerusalem, particularly the Catholic and the Orthodox.

The first station, at the Church of the Flagellation, is the starting point for processions to the Church of the Holy Sepulchre every Friday and for throngs of pilgrims on Good Friday.

The second station is at the remains of the Ecco Homo Arch. The arch takes its name from Pilate's words, "Behold the man." The arch, however, is a triumphal arch erected by Hadrian (A.D. 135) to celebrate the capture of Jerusalem. The right part of the arch is still preserved inside the Church of the Sisters of Zion.

The third station commemorates Christ's first fall on the Via Dolorosa.

The meeting between Jesus and Mary is commemorated at the fourth station.

At the fifth station an inscription memorializes the meeting between Jesus and Simon of Cyrene, who was given Christ's heavy cross to carry to Calvary.

The sixth station is dedicated to a meeting between Jesus and Veronica. This station illustrates how the sacred archaeology of Jerusalem has become a mixture of fact and fiction. There was no Veronica. In fact, her name is a made-up name that means "True Icon." The true icon is the image of Jesus, which allegedly was miraculously imprinted on the cloth with which Veronica wiped Jesus' face. This relic is kept in the Basilica of St. Peter in Rome. This scene appeared in the movie *The Passion of the Christ.*

A pillar at the seventh station marks Jesus' second fall.

At the eighth station, a small cross carved in the wall marks the point where Jesus met the women of Jerusalem.

The third fall of Jesus is commemorated by a Roman column at the ninth station.

The last five Stations of the Cross are situated inside the Church of the Holy Sepulchre.

The Stations of the Cross are a Catholic system of devotions. The original 14 stations from Jerusalem are reproduced at many Catholic pilgrimage sites and churches around the world. Sadly, the 14 stations are a mixture of fact and fiction and the devotionals that accompany them are heavy in salvation by works.

Church of the Holy Sepulchre

The tomb of Christ, which is located on the site of the Church of the Holy Sepulchre, was discussed in the chapter on burials, but this church, one of the most important in Christendom, is interesting in its own right. Most of the present structure is Crusader construction or later repairs. The church today is just a remnant of its past glory. A tour through the church today tells us more about the history of the competing factions of Eastern and Western Christianity than about the spirit of the gospel.

Entrance to the church is from a relatively small courtyard on the south through a single door into the south transept.

Just inside the entrance is the Stone of Anointing, believed to be the spot where Jesus' body was prepared for burial by Joseph of Arimathea. It is the 13th Station of the Cross. The lamps that hang over the stone are contributed by Armenians, Copts, Greeks, and Latins.

To the left, or west, of the entrance is the Rotunda of the Anastasis (Resurrection), the larger of the church's two domes. Under the center of the dome is the Edicule, the reconstruction of Christ's tomb (see the chapter on burials). The Edicule has two rooms. The entrance room holds the Angel's Stone, allegedly a fragment of the stone that sealed the tomb after Jesus' burial. The inner room is the tomb itself (or rather a remnant of it). The Eastern Orthodox, Roman Catholic, and Armenian churches all have rights to the interior of the tomb, and all three communities celebrate the liturgy or mass there daily. It is also used for other ceremonies on special occasions, such as the Holy Saturday ceremony of the Holy Fire celebrated by the Greek Orthodox Patriarch of Jerusalem.

Around the rotunda and other passageways (ambulatories) are many chapels dedicated to certain events or persons associated with the Passion, controlled by various factions of the church.

To the east of the Rotunda is the Catholicon, the Crusader structure housing the main altar of the church, today controlled by the Greek Orthodox. The second, smaller dome of the church directly over the center of this room marks the *omphalos* (the navel) of the world.

South of this, next to the entrance, is a stairway climbing to the top of the rock of Calvary (Golgotha), believed to be the site of Jesus' crucifixion. It is the most lavishly decorated part of the church. The main altar there, which belongs to the Greek Orthodox, has two windows that display the rock of Calvary (12th Station of the Cross). Beneath the altar there is a hole said to be the place where the cross was raised. The Roman Catholics have a rival altar to the side, the Chapel of the Nailing of the Cross (11th Station of the Cross). On the left of the altars, towards the Eastern Orthodox chapel, there is a statue of Mary believed to work miracles (13th Station of the Cross, where Jesus' body was removed from the cross and given to his family).

Beneath Calvary, on the main floor, is the Chapel of Adam. According to tradition, Jesus was crucified over the place where Adam's skull was buried. That is why medieval paintings of the crucifixion sometimes show blood from Christ's wounds flowing down onto a skull at the foot of the cross. The rock of Calvary can again be seen through a window on the altar wall. The crack in the rock is attributed to the earthquake that occurred when Jesus died on the cross.

At the bottom of a flight of stairs lies the subterranean Chapel of St. Helena, belonging to the Armenians. From there another set of 42 stairs leads down to the Roman Catholic Chapel of the Invention (Discovery) of the Holy Cross, believed to be the place where the True Cross was found by Helena on her pilgrimage to Jerusalem. This event is celebrated as a holy day in both the Eastern and Western churches.

I think that by now you have gotten the picture that this church is a battleground between the various sects of the Catholic and Orthodox churches. During the years when Jerusalem was under Turkish rule, the Roman Catholic and Orthodox churches sought to control the church by gaining favorable concessions from the Turkish government. The church is now regulated by a decree called the Status Quo, which establishes territorial rights and privileges among the squabbling churches.

The primary custodians are Eastern Orthodox, Armenian Apostolic, and Roman Catholic churches, with the Greek Orthodox

Church having the lion's share. The Coptic Orthodox, the Ethiopian Orthodox, and the Syriac Orthodox acquired lesser rights. Times and places of worship for each community are strictly regulated in common areas.

We can here mention only a few of the more notorious examples of conflict.

On a hot summer day in 2002, a Coptic monk, who was stationed on the roof to assert Coptic claims to the Ethiopian territory there, moved his chair from its agreed upon spot into the shade. This was interpreted as a hostile move by the Ethiopians, and 11 people were hospitalized after the resulting fracas. In another incident in 2004, during Orthodox celebrations of the Exaltation of the Holy Cross, a door to the Franciscan chapel was left open. This was taken as a sign of disrespect by the Orthodox, and a fistfight broke out. Some people were arrested, but no one was seriously injured. On Palm Sunday 2007, a fistfight broke out between Armenian and Greek monks when a Greek intruded on the Armenian celebration. In the ensuing melee, worshipers used their palm fronds to beat Israeli police who tried to intervene.

Under the Status Quo, no part of what is designated as common territory may be rearranged without consent from all communities. This often leads to the neglect of badly needed repairs when the communities cannot come to an agreement among themselves about the final shape of a project. Just such a disagreement has delayed the renovation of the Edicule, where the need of repair is now dire, but also where any change in the structure might result in a change to the Status Quo that would be unacceptable to one or more of the communities.

The most famous sign of this sad state of affairs is a ladder located on a window ledge over the church's entrance. As the story goes, someone placed a wooden ladder there sometime before 1852, when the Status Quo defined both the doors and the window ledges as common ground. The ladder remains there to this day because there is no agreement to move it.

None of the communities will entrust the others with the keys to the entrance. In 1192 the responsibility was assigned to two neighboring Muslim families. One family has the right to keep the keys. The other has the right to lock and unlock the door. Twice each day a member of the key-keeping family brings the keys to the door, which is then locked or unlocked by a member of the other family. Should we laugh or cry that the site of Christ's death has come to this?

BIBLIOGRAPHY

H. D. Lance, *The Old Testament and the Archeologist*, Fortress, 1981. The best simple overview of the problem of methodology and relating archaeology to the Bible.

John D. Currid, *Doing Archaeology in the Land of the Bible: A Basic Guide*, Baker, 1999. Quite elementary.

John Sailhamer, *Biblical Archaeology*, Zondervan, 1998. Very brief, no pictures. Evangelical.

Alfred J. Hoerth, *Archaeology and the Old Testament*, Baker, 1998. Evangelical overview of specific results.

John McRay, *Archaeology and the New Testament*, Baker, 1991. Evangelical overview of specific results.

Joseph P. Free, *Archaeology and Bible History*, revised and expanded by Howard F. Vos., Zondervan, 1992. Results by era. Evangelical. Dated.

Amihay Mazar, *Archaeology of the Land of the Bible, 10,000–586 B.C.E.*, Doubleday, 1990. More heavy-duty. Somewhat critical.

Amnon Ben-Tor, editor, *The Archaeology of Ancient Israel*, translated by R. Greenberg. Yale University Press, 1992. Somewhat critical.

J. Bartellt, *Cities of the Biblical World: Jericho*, Eerdmans, 1982. Evangelical.

Harold Mare, *The Archeology of Jerusalem*, Baker, 1987. Evangelical. Somewhat dated.

Hershel Shanks, *Jerusalem: An Archaeological Biography*, Biblical Archaeological Society, 1995.

Alfred J. Hoerth, Gerald L. Mattingly, and Edwin M. Yamauchi, editors, *Peoples of the Old Testament World*, Baker Books, 1994. Summaries on specific peoples.

J. Finegan, *The Archeology of the New Testament: The Life of Jesus and the Beginning of the Early Church*, Princeton, 1992.

E. Yamauchi, *The Archeology of N.T. Cities in Western Asia*, Baker, 1980.

REFERENCE WORKS

The Oxford Encyclopedia of Archaeology in the Near East, prepared under the auspices of the American Schools of Oriental Research; Eric M. Meyers, editor in chief. 1997, V1-5.

The New Encyclopedia of Archaeological Excavations in the Holy Land, Ephraim Stern, editor. Israel Exploration Society, 1993, V1-4 Best summary of sites. Volume 5 update.

GUIDE BOOKS

Jerome Murphy-O'Conner, *The Holy Land: An Archeological Guide*, Oxford, 1980, 1998.

PERIODICALS

POPULAR

**Biblical Archaeology Review*, somewhat critical, best pictures. Keeps up with recent finds and controversies.

Archeology and Biblical Research, most biblically oriented, apologetic, replaces *Bible and Spade.*

Biblical Illustrator, Southern Baptist Sunday School Teachers aid, disappointingly critical at times.

Biblical Archaeologist, more technical, now replaced by *Near Eastern Archaeology.*

PROFESSIONAL

Israel Exploration Journal

Tel Aviv

Bulletin of the American Schools of Oriental Research

OPPORTUNITIES

The Oriental Institute in Chicago is one of the best archaeological museums in the country.

The Field Museum in Chicago also has a good Egyptian section.

Metropolitan Museum of Art in New York is good on Egyptian material.

The University of Pennsylvania and Harvard also have important collections.

Unsurpassed, of course, are the Israel Museum and the Palestine Museum in Jerusalem. The British Museum in London and the Louvre in Paris are other important resources.

Excavation opportunities in Israel are announced each year in a winter or spring issue of *Biblical Archaeology Review.*

INDEX

C

D

E

T

U

V

W

Y

Z